Leveraging the
Wisdom of the Crowd
in Software Testing

BOOKS ON SOFTWARE AND SYSTEMS
DEVELOPMENT AND ENGINEERING
FROM AUERBACH PUBLICATIONS AND CRC PRESS

Adaptive, Dynamic, and Resilient Systems
Niranjan Suri and Giacomo Cabri (Editors)
ISBN 978-1-4398-6848-5

Agile Strategy Management: Techniques for Continuous Alignment and Improvement
Soren Lyngso
ISBN 978-1-4665-9607-8

Big Data, Mining, and Analytics: Components of Strategic Decision Making
Stephan Kudyba
ISBN 978-1-4665-6870-9

Big Data Analytics Strategies for the Smart Grid
Carol L. Stimmel
ISBN 978-1-4822-1828-2

Bursting the Big Data Bubble: The Case for Intuition-Based Decision Making
Jay Liebowitz (Editor)
ISBN 978-1-4822-2885-4

Buying, Supporting, Maintaining Software and Equipment: An IT Manager's Guide to Controlling the Product Lifecycle
Gay Gordon-Byrne
ISBN 978-1-4822-3278-3

BYOD for Healthcare
Jessica Keyes
ISBN 978-1-4822-1981-4

Case Studies in System of Systems, Enterprise Systems, and Complex Systems Engineering
Alex Gorod, Brian E. White, Vernon Ireland,
S. Jimmy Gandhi, and Brian Sauser (Editors)
ISBN 978-1-4665-0239-0

The CIO's Guide to Oracle Products and Solutions
Jessica Keyes
ISBN 978-1-4822-4994-1

Creating and Marketing New Products and Services
Rosanna Garcia
ISBN 978-1-4822-0360-8

Empowering Project Teams: Using Project Followership to Improve Performance
Marco Sampietro and Tiziano Villa
ISBN 978-1-4822-1755-1

Enterprise Integration and Information Architecture: A Systems Perspective on Industrial Information Integration
Li Da Xu
ISBN 978-1-4398-5024-4

The Essential Guide to Serial ATA and SATA Express
David A. Demming
ISBN 978-1-4822-4331-4

Formal Languages and Computation: Models and Their Applications
Alexander Meduna
ISBN 978-1-4665-1345-7

The Influential Project Manager: Winning Over Team Members and Stakeholders
Alfonso Bucero
ISBN 978-1-4665-9633-7

Introduction to Software Project Management
Adolfo Villafiorita
ISBN 978-1-4665-5953-0

Large Scale and Big Data: Processing and Management
Sherif Sakr and Mohamed Gaber (Editors)
ISBN 978-1-4665-8150-0

Mobile Social Networking and Computing: A Multidisciplinary Integrated Perspective
Yufeng Wang and Jianhua Ma
ISBN 978-1-4665-5275-3

Programming Languages for MIS: Concepts and Practice
Hai Wang and Shouhong Wang
ISBN 978-1-4822-2266-1

The SAP Materials Management Handbook
Ashfaque Ahmed
ISBN 978-1-4665-8162-3

Secure Data Provenance and Inference Control with Semantic Web
Bhavani Thuraisingham, Tyrone Cadenhead,
Murat Kantarcioglu, and Vaibhav Khadilka
ISBN 978-1-4665-6943-0

Zen of Cloud: Learning Cloud Computing by Examples on Microsoft Azure
Haishi Bai
ISBN 978-1-4822-1580-9

Leveraging the Wisdom of the Crowd in Software Testing

Mukesh Sharma
Rajini Padmanaban

CRC Press
Taylor & Francis Group
Boca Raton London New York

CRC Press is an imprint of the
Taylor & Francis Group, an **informa** business

AN AUERBACH BOOK

CRC Press
Taylor & Francis Group
6000 Broken Sound Parkway NW, Suite 300
Boca Raton, FL 33487-2742

First issued in paperback 2019

© 2015 by Taylor & Francis Group, LLC
CRC Press is an imprint of Taylor & Francis Group, an Informa business

No claim to original U.S. Government works

ISBN-13: 978-1-4822-5448-8 (hbk)
ISBN-13: 978-0-367-37834-9 (pbk)

Library of Congress Cataloging-in-Publication Data

Sharma, Mukesh (Software testing engineer)
    Leveraging the wisdom of the crowd in software testing / Mukesh Sharma, Rajini Padmanaban.
        pages cm
    Includes bibliographical references and index.
    ISBN 978-1-4822-5448-8 (hardback)
    1. Computer software--Testing--Data processing. 2. AskA services. 3. Internet research. I. Padmanaban, Rajini. II. Title.

QA76.76.T48S53 2014
005.3028'7--dc23   2014027273

Visit the Taylor & Francis Web site at
http://www.taylorandfrancis.com

and the CRC Press Web site at
http://www.crcpress.com

Contents

FOREWORD   ix

ACKNOWLEDGMENTS   xi

OVERVIEW   xiii

CHAPTER 1 INTRODUCING THE CROWD   1

What Is a Crowd?   2

History of Crowdsourcing   2

History of Crowdsourcing in Software Product Development   4

What Are the Traits of the Crowd That Make It Relevant
to Be Engaged in Various Stages of Product Development?   6

Did You Know?   9

CHAPTER 2 AN OVERVIEW INTO CROWDSOURCING   11

You Perform, We Provide the Platform   11

What Is Crowdsourcing?   11

Understanding the Varied Forms of Crowdsourcing   12

Crowd Creation   14

Crowd Voting   16

Crowd Wisdom   18

Crowd Funding   20

Is Crowdsourcing the Same as Outsourcing?   21

What Is Crowdsourced Testing and Where Does It Fit in
This Picture?   23

Understanding Crowdsourced Testing through Examples   27

The Rising Popularity of Crowdsourcing   29

Did You Know?   30

CHAPTER 3 WHY LEVERAGE THE CROWD FOR SOFTWARE
TESTING? 33
Are You Ready to Stand Out in a Crowd? 33
A Peek at Software Quality 33
Software Quality in the Current Day and Age 35
The Need for Alternate Solutions to Assure and Control
Software Quality 37
Tying the Gap in Quality to the Definition of
Crowdsourced Testing 38
A Case Study on Facebook Relevant in the World of Agile
Operations 39
Scenario 39
Challenges Posed by Scale 40
Solutioning 41
Summary 42
Leveraging Crowdsourced Testing in Various Testing Areas 42
Functional Testing 42
UI Testing 43
Usability Testing 43
Accessibility Testing 44
Performance Testing 44
Security Testing 45
Globalization Testing 45
Compatibility Testing 46
Did You Know? 47

CHAPTER 4 IS CROWDSOURCED TESTING A NO-BRAINER
SOLUTION TO ALL QUALITY PROBLEMS? 49
What Not to Crowdsource in Your Test Effort 51
Challenges and Limitations of a Crowdsourced Test Effort 55
Did You Know? 62

CHAPTER 5 HOW TO SUCCESSFULLY IMPLEMENT
CROWDSOURCED TESTING 63
Best Practices in Implementing a Successful Crowdsourced
Test Effort 64
When Do We Crowdsource Our Testing Effort? 65
What Do We Crowdsource in Our Testing Effort? 68
How Do We Crowdsource Our Testing Effort? 71
Examples: Practical Implementations of Crowdsourced Testing 75
Engagement Models in Leveraging a Crowdsourced Test Effort 82
Did You Know? 84

CHAPTER 6 DEFECT MANAGEMENT IN CROWDSOURCED
TESTING 85
What Is Defect Management? 85
What Are Some Core Challenges in Defect Management
in a Product Team? 86

Is Defect Management Any Different in a Crowdsourced
Test Effort?   90
What Can Go Wrong If Defect Management Is Not
Effective Specific to Crowdsourced Testing?   92
Can I Leverage Best Practices in Defect Management from
a Formal Testing Effort in My Crowdsourced Testing?   93
Are Defect Tracking and Measurement Important in
Crowdsourced Testing Too?   94
Are There Any Case Studies to Help Understand
Crowdsourced Testing Defect Management in Real Time?   95
Did You Know?   97

CHAPTER 7   WIN YOUR TEAM'S SUPPORT IN IMPLEMENTING
             CROWDSOURCED TESTING   99
             Did You Know?   108

CHAPTER 8   LET'S UNDERSTAND CROWDSOURCED TESTING
             HOLISTICALLY   111
Chapter 1: Introducing the Crowd   112
Chapter 2: An Overview into Crowdsourcing   112
Chapter 3: Why Leverage the Crowd for Software Testing?   113
Chapter 4: Is Crowdsourced Testing a No-Brainer Solution to
All Quality Problems?   114
Chapter 5: How to Successfully Implement Crowdsourced
Testing   115
Chapter 6: Defect Management in Crowdsourced Testing   116
Chapter 7: Win Your Team's Support in Implementing
Crowdsourced Testing   117
Chapter 8: Let's Understand Crowdsourced Testing Holistically 118
Additional Myths and Facts   119
Is Crowdsourced Testing a Viable Career to Build?   120
Who Can Become a Crowdsourced Tester?   120
What Should I Do to Prepare and Be Successful in
Crowdsourced Testing Assignments?   122
Did You Know?   127

CHAPTER 9   FUTURE OF CROWDSOURCED TESTING   131
Sizing the Crowdsourcing Industry   131
Future of Crowdsourced Testing   133
Market Trends   135
Business Trends   137
Technology Trends   139
End User Trends   140
Did You Know?   142

CHAPTER 10   BUILDING AN ECOSYSTEM AROUND
             CROWDSOURCED TESTING   143
Crowd Testers   145
Crowd Seekers   145

The Platform   146
Common Knowledge Repository on Crowdsourced Testing   148
Tools to Help with the Crowdsourced Testing Effort   149
Who Is Responsible for Building This Ecosystem?   150
What to Watch for as We Let the Ecosystem Develop   151
Did You Know?   151

REFERENCES   153
INDEX   157

Foreword

Thousands of years of history, dating back to the Paleolithic Era, have taught humans the value of working together. Several strong warriors were required to work together to bring down a wooly mammoth for food and clothing. Specialists needed to learn how to grow food or pray for crops, while others depended on their talents. Human history is full of examples of people working together to overcome seemingly insurmountable challenges. The building of the Great Pyramid of Giza or the Temples of Ancient Greece, curating the Hanging Gardens of Babylon, constructing the Freedom Tower in New York City through the accuracy of Wikipedia and the richness of Twitter and Facebook—all of these amazing accomplishments in human history came to be only because of the coordinated work of many. In my own home many years ago, the phrase "many hands makes light work" was met with groans, as it was shorthand for "kids help out with chores." However, as we have entered a 21st century with ubiquitous connectivity and an "always on" mentality, the idea of everyone being available to contribute some of their discretionary time to a common cause is not too far-fetched. In fact, it's becoming the norm. We saw the rise of SMS displaced temporarily by Farmville updates, and then on to WhatsApp, SnapChat, Instagram and Pinterest. People working together to share information and improve each other's lives through a collective effort. While it may be premature to dismiss

Garret Hardin's Tragedy of the Commons – in which individuals act selfishly contrarian to the best interests of a group – it's safe to say that technology has leveled the playing field and enabled a more collaborative model of collective contribution where everyone can "win" in their own unique way.

There are thousands of examples throughout human history to illustrate the value of a diverse group of people focused on a challenge. If we were to pore through that hypothetical list, I would imagine that much time would elapse before software testing came in to view. Fortunately, Mukesh and Rajini have done the heavy lifting to create a framework for all of us to use to successfully apply these collaborative crowdsourcing techniques to improve the quality of our software. This book is unique in explaining how to combine the power of crowdsourcing with the craft of software testing to share practical experience, lessons learned, and provide guidance for others to hit the ground running. The rich set of examples provided here helps set the context for all practitioners to help improve understanding of a fast moving field. The depth of experience comes through with guidance on how to build a platform, create an ecosystem, and avoid the many potential problems and pitfalls that present a threat to successful crowdsource testing initiatives. The Did-You-Know conclusion offers pragmatic suggestions and offers a synopsis of advice to move forward on crowdsourced testing.

Quality is an amorphous, ephemeral condition, especially in software—and very hard to achieve in an increasingly online and mobile world. High quality requires meeting the needs and requirements of a broad and diverse set of people—and to do so requires a diverse set of analysts—a crowd—to help ensure everyone's needs are met. This book offers a formula for helping everyone be successful in leveraging the crowd to improve the quality of the software experience.

Ross Smith
Director of Test, Skype Division, Microsoft

Acknowledgments

We thank the following people and teams who have helped us make this book possible: Ross Smith, Director of Test at Microsoft Corporation, was an essential resource. We have been fortunate to discuss and brainstorm various crowdsourced testing ideas with him over the past 2 years. He has not only patiently read through the entire content of this book and provided his valuable feedback and endorsement but has also been a great supporter of this testing concept, including implementing it at Microsoft in varied forms. He has thus contributed to the world of crowdsourced testing through his practitioner experience, and we are so glad that he has shared those experiences with us and let us quote them in this book. Thank you, Ross!

The crowdsourced testing project management team at QA InfoTech, spearheaded by our CTO, Kunal Chauhan, has also provided several of the hands-on details and implementation best practices we have mentioned in this book. His team, especially some of our test managers, such as Ashwin Arora, Gaurav Sidana, and Mayank Upadhyay, continues to work with the community at large in helping the crowdsourced testing practice mature at QA InfoTech, and all of that learning has been valuable for us to reference in this book in various places. Thanks team and continue your great work in helping crowdsourced testing evolve not just at QA InfoTech but also in the industry at large.

We also want to mention and thank the accessibility testing team at QA InfoTech, which works with visually challenged users in testing our clients' products for accessibility. They were one of the early implementers of crowdsourced testing at QA InfoTech, which made us strongly believe that crowdsourced testing can manifest itself in multiple ways. Our thanks to Gautam Gupta and his team for their proactive measures on this front, which we have shared with you in this book in several places. We also thank our marketing manager, Saurabh Ganguly, who has helped behind the scenes with this book at varied times and in varied ways.

Finally, we also thank the SQE community (www.sqe.com) for seeing the value in this topic and inviting Mukesh and me to present this at their conferences in the United States, three times in a row, both as conference sessions and as tutorials. The reception shown by the community at the conference has been a major source of motivation for us to write this book.

To QA InfoTech's clients and partners worldwide, thank you for the opportunity to work alongside you to help bring the very best in software to market. Our experience in working with such high-caliber professionals continues to inspire us to strive to make our collaborations the very best they can be.

To QA InfoTech's global team, thank you for your commitment to excellence and quality. You are the engineers whom new testers should model as they learn our industry. We are very proud of what we've accomplished together and look forward to what the future holds.

Overview

Many hands make light work.

None of us is as smart as all of us.

The market is always right.

These statements very succinctly reflect the sentiment of this book on leveraging the wisdom of the crowd in software testing. Crowdsourcing practices across domains can be traced back at least three centuries. Although it is such an age-old practice, it started taking formal shape in its current name only in the last decade, thanks to the penetration of the Internet, social technologies, the agile style of development, mobile and cloud computing, and the application-intensive software development focus. The crowdsourcing market was estimated to be US$500 million in 2011 and was projected to have an approximately 75% growth over 2010. Over two thirds of this growth was attributed to Internet services, media, entertainment, and technology.[1]

Global outreach, quick time to market, and a feature-rich design are some of the major drivers in today's market in determining a product's success. Product companies are constantly on the lookout for innovative development and testing techniques to take charge of these driving forces. One such paradigm software testing technique gaining popularity is crowdsourced testing. The scale, flexibility, cost-effectiveness, and fast turnaround it has to offer are all being spoken about at length, in several forums. While there are some resources online to refer to, on what crowd testing is all about and how to leverage it, there is no one comprehensive book as of today on crowdsourced testing that talks about practices, case studies, and the future of this technique. This book is intended to fill that void and serve as the go-to material for anyone wanting to leverage the wisdom of the crowd in software testing.

Specifically, while there are several online resources to understand the concept of crowdsourcing and examples of how it works in its various forms, there aren't formal resources to guide a tester, a test team, or a management team on what it takes to implement crowdsourcing in a software testing effort. We have been researching a lot on this area at QA InfoTech, presenting our experiences in conferences such as StarEast and StarWest and implementing crowdsourced testing for our clients at relevant places to supplement the core team's testing efforts. All of these together have been a major source of inspiration to write this book, which will serve as a practical guide for anyone wanting to adopt crowdsourcing for their software testing needs. The book is comprehensive enough to talk about the history of crowdsourcing and crowdsourced testing, implementation practices, and future trends. It provides the reader with a holistic and practical view of the topic and talks about building a career in this space. Since it also covers future trends, this material will be applicable for readers into the future as well. As practitioner's in the software testing discipline, we hope to bring out in this book our experiences, including some niche points such as defect management specific to crowdsourced testing and building a career in crowdsourced testing, which we have gained over the years through hands-on implementation. The book is divided into 10 chapters, and in this overview, you will read a brief outline of what is covered in each of them.

Chapter 1: Introducing the Crowd

Crowd forms the crux of this book. *Leverage the Wisdom of the Crowd in Software Testing* starts off defining who forms the crowd and why the crowd is of particular interest to us. It then talks about the history or timeline of when the crowd gained significance and how books such as *Leveraging the Wisdom of Crowds* have been instrumental in helping the industry understand this concept. It also talks about the history of crowdsourcing in the software product development world and the core characteristics or traits of a crowd that make it very valuable in this domain. Setting this baseline early on in the book is important to help you gradually move into understanding the scope of crowdsourcing and specifically crowdsourced testing.

Chapter 2: An Overview into Crowdsourcing

This chapter takes you from understanding what forms a crowd to understanding what crowdsourcing is. It talks about the definition of crowdsourcing, the surge in popularity of this concept, the varied forms of crowdsourcing with intuitive examples, and introduces you to crowdsourced testing. As part of crowdsourced testing, it also gives examples to help you understand the practical implementation.

Chapter 3: Why Leverage the Crowd for Software Testing?

From this chapter on, the book starts focusing heavily on crowd-sourced testing. In this chapter, specifically, we talk about where quality stands as of today and why crowdsourced testing is relevant to the world of software quality at this time, as opposed to a few years back or a few years into the future. In this context, we also discuss a case study from Facebook on how it works with the crowd on an ongoing basis to test for its updates and new features. The focus also is on talking about various test attributes (functional, performance, security, globalization, compatibility, usability, accessibility, etc.) and discusses how crowdsourced testing is relevant to each of them.

Chapter 4: Is Crowdsourced Testing a No-Brainer Solution to All Quality Problems?

Crowdsourced testing, while very powerful and effective, has its own limitations, like any other solution. This chapter talks about the challenges, limitations, and situations when crowdsourced testing will not work. These constraints could be from technology, logistics, or effectiveness angles. Understanding these is important, as they form our problem statement for implementing an effective solution that will be discussed in subsequent chapters.

Chapter 5: How to Successfully Implement Crowdsourced Testing?

Having talked about the constraints in leveraging crowdsourced testing, this chapter is the core and essence of the book, as it talks about how to successfully implement a crowdtest effort. It talks about best practices in implementation, answering several questions such as what, when, and how to crowdsource, in a test effort. It covers best practices in mitigating the constraints and challenges discussed earlier, including solutions such as a crowdsourcing platform that can be built to test software products in the cloud. Several case studies that discuss how crowdsourced testing was adopted in both product and services companies are elaborated on in this chapter. We also look at the various engagement models in which crowdsourced testing can be implemented.

Chapter 6: Defect Management in Crowdsourced Testing

Defect management is a beast of its own in software quality engineering. It makes or breaks the quality of the product and the reputation of the test team. While defect management has its own challenges even in a centralized test team, one can only imagine what it would entail in a crowdsourced test effort, where the team is most often de-centralized and does not have insights into the team's executional practices. This chapter solely addresses effective defect management in crowdsourced testing, discussing how to keep the effort simple yet effective so it is a win-win situation for both the crowd and the test organization.

Chapter 7: Win Your Team's Support in Implementing Crowdsourced Testing

A test team, although convinced about crowdsourced testing, can face hurdles in implementing it at various levels—from its stakeholders, from other team members, from end users, etc. This chapter focuses on identifying such blocks and how to successfully win team's confidence in implementing a crowdsourced test effort. This is a process that might take time and several iterations. The overhead may also be high, all the way from talking with the stakeholders to addressing their concerns to doing pilots to convince them on sample results that the effort can yield. However, without the support of the stakeholders, a crowdsourced test effort may not even take off or may fail miserably even in areas where it can potentially scale well. Given the importance of this activity, one full chapter has been dedicated to this topic.

Chapter 8: Let's Understand Crowdsourced Testing Holistically

By now, after reading through the first seven chapters, you will have a very detailed idea on what crowdsourced testing is all about and how to implement it successfully. This chapter serves as a wrap-up note helping the tester step back from all the details and look at the landscape holistically to differentiate myths from facts and emerge with a clear understanding of crowdsourced testing. You will be able to draw the distinction by now as to what is a myth and what is a fact. This chapter also touches upon career opportunities that an individual has as a crowd tester, which will help you make useful and critical choices in one's career progression in the field of software testing. Thus, this chapter will serve as a refresher/summary helping you look back on the information from each chapter and serving as a useful guide into career planning in the field of crowdsourced testing.

Chapter 9: Future of Crowdsourced Testing

We get close to wrapping up this guide to crowdsourced testing by talking about the future of this area. Herein we look at who can leverage this technique—service companies, product companies, the general public, etc., what to expect in terms of trends in this area moving forward (say, two to three years down the line), what technologies will continue to give this practice its required facelift, and the forecasted market size of crowdsourcing and crowdsourced testing. Through this chapter, you will get not just a detailed understanding on implementing a crowdsourced test effort, but more importantly, a view into both the business and the engineering aspects of crowdsourced testing.

Chapter 10: Building an Ecosystem around Crowdsourced Testing

While all along in this book, you will have gained comprehension of what crowdsourced testing is and how to implement it in a project, this chapter, the conclusion, is slightly offbeat. Herein, we look at the need to build a crowdsourced testing ecosystem, who the players of such an ecosystem would be, and who would need to champion such an effort of building an ecosystem. This ecosystem is in itself a futuristic trend, and given its importance, we have dedicated one chapter to it. Given the scale and reach of crowdsourced testing, its value can further be maximized by building an ecosystem that brings together the crowd testers, seekers, a platform, a knowledge repository, and the right tools. That is the core focus of this chapter, gearing you to become an active participant in the development of such an ecosystem and getting you excited about the future of this discipline.

1

INTRODUCING THE CROWD

Before the beginning of great brilliance, there must be chaos. Before a brilliant person begins something great, they must look foolish in the crowd.[2]

Software is no new term in the current-day world. It has evolved to revolutionize every discipline, both at an enterprise level and at a common man level. Technologies, engineering practices, team engagement, and collaboration models have continued to change over time to adapt to the need of the day, to bring in optimized solutions in delivering software on time, within the defined budget, and of exceptional quality.

As engineering practices evolve, so have the software testing practices that form a significant part of the larger set of development efforts. Software testing has been exposed to a lot of challenges in the last decade—if we were to see these challenges as opportunities, the scale, scope, tool set, and team level visibility of the testing discipline have increased manifold. Testing has had to keep pace with the newer technologies that the product team adopts and understand how they might impact testing to devise a holistic test strategy from manual and automated testing fronts. Testing teams are engaged in the product life cycle much earlier than they used to be, testing for functionality and compatibility across supported platforms; areas such as accessibility and usability are getting a lot more attention; globalization is an important piece of the testing pie; security now extends beyond the basic web application testing level. All of these have opened a whole new window of opportunities for the testing team to align with the rest of the product team.

As we talk about the changes in the software development world, one noticeable new change that the industry is embracing in recent years is "leveraging the crowd," be it in product design, development, or testing. To establish our baseline and a common understanding, let us focus in this chapter on what we mean by the term *crowd*, the history of both crowdsourcing in general and crowdsourcing in product development, and the traits of a crowd that make it relevant to be engaged at various stages in the software engineering process.

What Is a Crowd?

There are varied definitions of this term that are floated around these days, especially after the term *crowdsourcing* became popular. While we will look at the varied forms of crowd and align them with the forms of crowdsourcing in subsequent chapters, we will herein look at a very simple definition of *crowd* to introduce the group to you. A crowd is a gathering of people, of varying numbers, who act in an extempore and independent manner. They are not necessarily tied to any organization, do not have any special accreditations, and typically lack organization. However, the term *crowd* could also be used to refer to a group of people with a common trait or characteristic. The origin of this word dates back to the year 1275 and has been a commonly used word since then. A few examples of using this term in a statement include:

- A crowd has gathered in front of the shopping mall.
- The elated crowd cheered the singer at the show.
- There was a large crowd from Berkeley in the SFO downtown to watch the fireworks.

The term *crowd* can also be used to refer to a group of things, though this is not a very common case in regular usage. For example:

- A crowd of new shops have opened in the Great American Mall in Phoenix.
- The marketplace is crowded with advertisements of various brands.

The word *crowd* is thus used in both its noun and verb forms to refer to both animate and inanimate objects to describe a large number of a certain thing.

History of Crowdsourcing

As you read this book, you will be interested in knowing that the term *crowdsourcing* is now officially part of the *Oxford Dictionary*.[3]

The term *crowdsourcing* is relatively new; it started gaining attention in 2006 when Jeff Howe coined this term in his article "The Rise of Crowdsourcing." Looking back at the history of the activity involved in crowdsourcing, which is leveraging the crowd to source information or solve a problem, the concept has been in practice long before the term started gaining popularity or use, in the current-day technology world. For example, one source dates the use of crowdsourcing to 1714,[4] when the British government announced a prize for anyone who could reliably calculate longitude. This article also cites other examples, including a competition in France initiated by King Louis IV for making alkali from sea salt. In the 19th century, the *Oxford Dictionary* used a crowd (of about 800 users) to catalog its words. All of these examples clearly show how crowdsourcing has been in use in varied countries and forms to solve issues that merely could not be done in-house with a team of experts.

In 2004, crowdsourcing started getting a lot of attention globally when James Surowiecki wrote a book called *The Wisdom of Crowds*. This is a very interesting book and one of the highly suggested reading materials for anyone who is new to crowdsourcing. As one of the early books written on this topic, this is still an authority in understanding why and how the crowd's collective intelligence is important in solving problems. James presents a lot of interesting examples in his book to explain the concept of crowd wisdom, but his introductory case on the weight of the ox is more than sufficient to summarize his case in point. He talks about an exercise where Francis Galton, in 1907, leveraged the crowd to find an ox's weight. Galton had 800 people guessing the weight of an ox after it was slaughtered. Of the 787 valid entries that he received, the average weight of the ox turned out to be 1197 pounds, while the actual weight was indeed very close, at 1198 pounds. This is a starter case with which James talks about the collective wisdom of the crowd and how it surpasses even individual inputs from experts (in this case, estimates from individual cattle experts). This book from James followed by the article from Jeff Howe created a lot of buzz for crowdsourcing between 2004 and 2006. This base they created has been instrumental in experimenting with the use of crowdsourcing in several domains and for a multitude of uses in the last eight years.

In case you wonder whether the examples quoted by James Surowiecki are the only ones that are backed by testimony of the power and wisdom of the crowd, there are other examples too to mention here. Recently, Gideon Rosenblatt, who was reading *The Wisdom of Crowds*, was inspired to try a similar exercise to validate the cases that James was talking about. He kicked off an exercise similar to guessing the weight of the ox—this time it was guessing the number of cereal pieces in a glass vase full of them.[5] Gideon leveraged the social computing technologies to reach out to the crowd in conducting his experiment; in this case, he used Google+. After an initial short trial with about 500 guesses, he increased the limits and got a total of 2238 valid guesses. He conducted the experiment one more time with a clearer image to ensure he was able to collect results that were reliable. The second time around he got 436 valid guesses. On analyzing the results further, he concluded that the median number of cereal pieces guessed by the first set of participants turned out to be 402, while from the second experiment the result was 450. The exact number of cereal pieces in the vase was 467. While the numbers here are not as precise as what they turned out to be back in 1907 when the ox weight guessing event happened, this additionally adds to our underlying school of thought over the course of this book that the collective wisdom of the crowd can be very powerful in eliciting answers, solving problems if the factors within which the crowd works are conducive to help them bring out their best. We will talk about those factors in detail in our subsequent chapters, but these examples will help form your base in understanding the power of the crowd.

History of Crowdsourcing in Software Product Development

In the previous section, we saw examples of how crowdsourcing has long existed before the term gained popularity and visibility among the masses. They were all practical problems that needed to be solved to create value to the general public or studies that were taken up to prove the power of the crowd. But what is the history of crowdsourcing in the world of software product development?

Beta testing is a very popular instance of crowdsourced testing. If we look at the history of beta testing, it dates back to the 1950s when IBM first coined this term to perform hardware testing at the second level—a level outside of the team that develops the product. While IBM dropped usage of this term in the 1960s, the term had already taken such deep roots that several organizations started using it. So, in one sense the use of crowdsourcing, specifically crowd testing in the hardware world, started with IBM, making its way into the software world too. To this day, it is a strongly suggested and used testing technique to get product feedback from a select group of end users who have the domain knowledge and prior experience using the product's earlier versions. Beta programs were conducted not just for testing a built software to find existing defects, but also to get end user suggestions to incorporate in subsequent releases. The year that James released his book *The Wisdom of Crowds* Gartner published a report that Microsoft (specifically Windows) is the biggest beta tester in history.

So, while we are able to map the origins of crowd testing to the beta programs, how did crowd development efforts start? Herein, it is worth briefly looking at the history of open-source software development. The freeware programs started in the software world in the early 1980s when the free software movement was launched. It would interest you to know that even before the free software phase, open-source software existed in its own shape and form dating back to the 1950s. During this period, any software that was created was based on the principles of openness, where the source code would be distributed along with the software, empowering organizations to make code changes as needed to create functional software that aligns with their hardware and operating system (OS) needs. If we look at this in the current-day information technology jargon, open-source software was encouraged back then to allow organizations to take on the professional services activity themselves. So, this can be looked at as the origin of crowdsourcing in the software development world.

In all direct reference to the open-source movement, it started taking shape with the introduction of Linux in 1991. Linux is a very popular example of crowdsourcing in software development to this day and how volunteer developers work on contributing to the code base on an ongoing basis. While the work done as part of the Linux projects have a direct mapping to crowdsourcing from our viewpoint, it wasn't until 1998, when the Open Source Initiative was initiated, that this movement gained formal recognition.

From an implementation standpoint, these events give us a sense that crowdsourcing in the product development world, be it in the design, development, or testing phases, has existed since the 1950s, although it started getting formal recognition only in the last decade. And while organizations have leveraged it in possible ways over the last decade, there is still quite some ambiguity, fear of the unknown, lack of overall buy-in, need for better proof that crowdsourcing can be leveraged for a varied set of scenarios, etc., that still limit the industry-wide official acceptance of this concept. This book will be a step in that direction, de-mystifying a lot of such open questions and providing clarity with live examples of how organizations have benefited from crowdsourcing, specifically crowdsourced testing, encouraging better industry-wide acceptance and application of this concept in the coming years.

What Are the Traits of the Crowd That Make It Relevant to Be Engaged in Various Stages of Product Development?

The term *crowd* is magical—it has a simple meaning, but the power of the crowd is extremely high. A typical user of a product is also part of a crowd when you look at the overall group of end users. To that effect, if we were to look at the traits of a crowd that make it relevant to engage in product development (be it in the design, development, content creation, or testing stages), the following core points emerge:

End user mind-set: The crowd can be gathered from a part of the organization or from a representative base of end users, external to the organization. Depending on the type of product/application that is being built, if it is from an external representative user base, it brings very rich criteria to the table, which is the end user mind-set. This is a trait that the organization cannot match even if it brings the most expensive testers on board. For example, an organization that is building a K–12 math software decides to go to a nearby school, to have a crowd of students and teachers use the product for a specific period of time and provide feedback. The richness and practicality in the feedback from, say, a second-grader may not be matched by even a test architect on the team, given that the second-grader is a realistic end user.

This feedback from representative end users is used not just at the testing phase, but should more importantly be included in the subsequent planning and design phases as well, to build a product that aligns with end user needs.

Subject matter expertise: The crowd can be a group of people with the required subject matter expertise in working on a product to address the team's constraints, including lack of very specific subject matter experts and lack of time and budget to handle everything in-house. While one would expect the internal team to build the required subject matter expertise in building a product, it is not always feasible to have a fully staffed team working on the project at all times. There may be situations where experts are not available, finding the right expert may be an issue, and it may not make financial sense to have the expert in-house for the entire duration of the project. The crowd is a sought-after solution in such cases since one can find the right crowd on an on-demand basis to address the organization's domain expertise needs. For example, let's say an organization in North America is building a global product and has created localized versions of its solution. It does not have the right expertise to verify the content in specific languages, for example, Balinese. The requirement here may not be long term, but verifying the content before product release is an important step to ensure overall product success. Given the trait of the crowd where the representative group of people has the required subject matter expertise in this case, the crowd is a very relevant solution to leverage. Similarly, the crowd can be a community of open-source developers. For example, Linux is a popular case of community-contributed code for the open-source operating system. The crowd herein has very rich subject matter expertise that is helping it contribute to the source code development as well as code verification.

The testing attitude: This trait of the crowd is specifically aligned to the product's testing needs. Every user (that together forms the crowd), when chosen as a representative base for a product, will bring an important element of the testing attitude to the table. For example, if you are an avid smartphone user, you will have inherent traits of a tester in the smartphone market, such as the ones below:

A thirst to understand how things work: You will be interested in knowing how things work, and to understand this, you will play around with the product proactively, think of ways to improve user experience, share your thoughts in relevant forums, be excited about opportunities where you can beta test the product, etc. This analysis mind-set often makes the crowd a great testing team.

A sense of inquisitiveness/curiosity: In line with the point above, the crowd is a curious bunch of people that wants to understand what options are available in the market, what features are coming out in the next release, how this product fares against competition, etc. Such curiosity makes the crowd a very valuable group of people with a testing mind-set in evaluating the product.

An enhanced set of observations: The crowd typically does not have full visibility into the system's internals. As an external group that validates and verifies the product or rather uses the product from realistic end user angles, the product team is able to elicit a more enhanced set of observations than what it could generate from within the team.

A questioning mind-set: This is a trait in succession to how things work and the curiosity pieces discussed above. The crowd typically has a questioning mind-set, where it does not want to accept anything at face value. It wants to question claims made by an organization, which is a great trait for eliciting better and richer product feedback. For example, the organization may make claims about the performance of a product, its page load time, response time, etc. The crowd will not rely on these numbers. It will actually gauge what the product performance is, at run time, to determine whether it is acceptable or not.

Using crowdsourcing in software product development is only a part of the overall pie. Crowdsourcing stretches itself into various other forms/facets in engaging with users in solving a range of problems. The examples we discussed in this chapter, especially around the history of crowdsourcing, give us an understanding of the early use of crowdsourcing to solve community problems and invent new solutions. In continuation to those, in the current day, we have specific forms of crowdsourcing that are leveraged not just to benefit software organizations, but more importantly to bring in the crowd to help create solutions that are important to the community—for example, in areas such as education, healthcare, societal uplift, etc. These are the forms and the varied manifestations of crowdsourcing that we will see in Chapter 2, which will also then set the base for us to start delving into the specifics of crowdsourced testing.

Did You Know?[D-1,D-2]

- Crowdsourcing is also referred to by other names, such as *fan sourcing*, *crowd casting*, *open sourcing*, and *mass collaboration*.
- Examples of who uses crowdsourcing include Amazon, Netflix, Wikipedia, and DuPont.
- Estimates say that about 1 million workers have been paid $1–2 billion for crowdsourcing projects.
- A crowdsourcing contest for Coca-Cola's energy drink brand, Burn, yielded 135 rich video entries in just 5 weeks. Here are its tips for successful crowd content creation:
  - Don't plan for a viral campaign.
  - Do it with consumers.
  - Aim for strong emotional reactions.
  - Seed! Don't wait for people to discover it.
  - Create a consistent and shareable experience.
- Get your timing right.

2

AN OVERVIEW INTO CROWDSOURCING

You Perform, We Provide the Platform

We looked at what a crowd is in Chapter 1. Although the focus of this book is crowdsourced testing, crowdsourcing has a much larger meaning that we should understand. Crowdsourcing is growing leaps and bounds in its scope and reach, given the growth in technology that facilitates putting together a crowdsourced team. Crowdsourced testing is only a subset of the larger crowdsourcing umbrella.

What Is Crowdsourcing?

There is no one universal definition for the term *crowdsourcing*; however, there are zillions of definitions that float online on what this term means, as it has a very simple and intuitive meaning based on its name and the activities it entails. Some of the more popular definitions include the following:

Crowdsourcing is the practice of obtaining needed services, ideas, or content by soliciting contributions from a large group of people, and especially from an online community, rather than from traditional employees or suppliers.[6]

Jeff Howe defines it as "the act of a company or institution taking a function once performed by employees and outsourcing it to an undefined (and generally large) network of people in the form of an open call. This can take the form of peer-production (when the job is performed collaboratively), but is also often undertaken by sole individuals. The crucial prerequisite is the use of the open call format and the large network of potential laborers."[7]

Enrique Estellés-Arolas and Fernando González Ladrón-de-Guevara's definition of crowdsourcing, after reviewing and consolidating over 40 definitions, is as follows:

> Crowdsourcing is a type of participative online activity in which an individual, an institution, a non-profit organization, or company proposes to a group of individuals of varying knowledge, heterogeneity, and number, via a flexible open call, the voluntary undertaking of a task. The undertaking of the task, of variable complexity and modularity, and in which the crowd should participate bringing their work, money, knowledge and/or experience, always entails mutual benefit. The user will receive the satisfaction of a given type of need, be it economic, social recognition, self-esteem, or the development of individual skills, while the crowdsourcer will obtain and utilize to their advantage what the user has brought to the venture, whose form will depend on the type of activity undertaken.[8]

Another simple definition of crowdsourcing reads: "Crowdsourcing is the practice of obtaining needed services, ideas, or content by soliciting contributions from a large group of people, and especially from an online community, rather than from traditional employees or suppliers." We have taken this definition from Wikipedia[9] for the simple reason that Wikipedia itself is an excellent example of successful crowdsourcing, where the crowd voluntarily contributes to the content.

If we were to draw the true essence of crowdsourcing and put it very simply, it is nothing but a set of tasks that are completed by a large group of people external to the core team. The tasks can be very diverse in nature, all the way from development to testing to getting the crowd's input through their votes, having the crowd solve problems, encouraging them to fund for specific projects, etc. But at a high level the definition is very simple, where the main phrases to remember are "set of tasks," "large group of people," and "external to the core team."

Understanding the Varied Forms of Crowdsourcing

Crowdsourcing, when put to implementation in the real world, can take varied forms, depending on how it is put to use. This is where the set of tasks we talk about in the crowdsourcing definition come into play.

Depending on the type of task that we engage the crowd for, crowdsourcing can largely take up one of the following forms:

1. Crowd creation
2. Crowd voting
3. Crowd wisdom
4. Crowd funding

These don't necessarily form an exhaustive list of all of crowdsourcing, as this is a relatively new technique in the IT field that is continuing to evolve by the day. However, the list is large enough to give you a comprehensive meaning of crowdsourcing and empower you to leverage and customize each of the listed items for your individual project needs. Let us look at each of these crowdsourcing types in detail with examples. But before we do that, we need to understand one additional point: crowd motivators. When you engage a crowd to do a task, they are not really your employees. There is often no legal binding that you have, in working with them. There are some exceptions here, though in terms of a nondisclosure agreement (NDA) that can be signed with a specific crowd, especially when a private beta effort is in progress. Terms and conditions may be laid out especially around code of conduct of the crowd, but enforcing any violation legally is often so much more difficult in crowdsourcing as opposed to an insourced or an outsourced project. So, if the crowd is not directly your employee base, what is its motivation in working for you? The motivators can be varying in nature—they could be monetary returns, curiosity and interest in a company's products and direction, community participation, brand loyalty, sense of inclusion and transparency in a company's products, or simply pure fun. More than one factor could also motivate the crowd. Crowd motivators are an important element to understand, and we will touch upon this in multiple places over the course of this book. The reason we introduce this element now is that as we move on to understanding the crowdsourcing types, we will look at the following five elements for each of them:

1. The definition of the crowdsourcing type
2. Common uses
3. Who benefits from this model
4. What are the crowd motivators
5. Popular examples implemented under this type of crowdsourcing

We will look at very basic and intuitive definitions from a theory standpoint and delve into the meaning through examples.

Crowd Creation

As the name suggests, this type of crowdsourcing leverages the crowd to create content. The content can be anything to meet the needs of the person requesting it to be created—it could be content specific to be used on a company's products and portals, or it can be something as complex as code that is developed open source. For the sake of simplicity, even code is considered content in this case. Crowd creation comes in very handy when the subject matter expertise of the crowd is valuable regardless of the domain you operate in. Some areas where this is commonly used include software development, translations, and photography, and in all these areas, the crowd creates content that will be consumed either by organizations or by the crowd themselves. If you look at motivating factors, these typically include money, fun, and commitment to a certain organization that drives the crowd to create content. So, what could be relevant examples from our current-day world that we can relate to, in this case? Linux is a very popular one where the crowd creates code on an evolving basis. iStockPhoto is another widely known case, where the crowd shares its content (photographs in this case), which is then consumed either by organizations or by the crowd. Similarly, 99designs is another great example where organizations invite the crowd to submit designs that they can use for varied purposes. A common scenario here is for organizations to leverage the crowd to design their logos. This is a very effective model, especially in the case of start-ups that want to have a good set of design options to choose from but at the same time do not have the required funds to engage expensive professional designers.

Pictorially, seen below are a couple of good examples of crowd creation, from companies such as Ben & Jerry's and Dunkin' Donuts, where they invite the crowd to give them input on new flavors they would like to see from these companies (Figure 2.1). This feedback the crowd provides is invaluable in their process of deciding new flavors, as it comes directly from the end users. This kind of feedback would be very difficult for companies to collect, even if they were to hire expensive product designers (Figure 2.2).

Figure 2.1 Ben & Jerry's—a real-world example of crowd creation.[32]

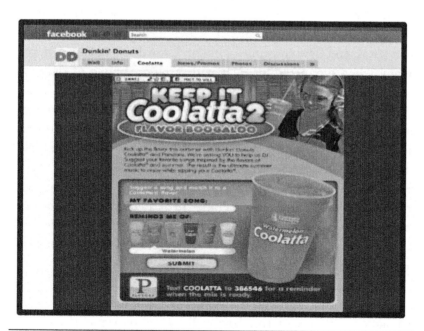

Figure 2.2 Dunkin' Donuts—a real-world example of crowd creation.[33]

These newer techniques are more feasible in the current day, thanks to the growth in the social computing world, mobile world, and infrastructure world—be it the cloud offerings, using applications such as Facebook or LinkedIn, wherein the company or person seeking input from the crowd has a platform to connect with them, and finally, the mind-boggling growth of mobile devices and the applications built for mobile devices, which make crowdsourcing very feasible for all entities involved. This holds true not just for crowd creation, but all forms of crowdsourcing that follow over the next few sections.

Crowd Voting

All of these crowdsourcing techniques are very straightforward in deciphering the meaning they hold. As the name suggests, this is one where the crowd is invited to vote on specific questions, polls, and surveys that an organization or an individual has triggered. According to Jeff Howe, the person who coined the term *crowdsourcing*, this is the most popular of its varied manifestations. He talks about a 1:10:89 rule, in which 1% of the crowd creates, 10% votes, and 89% consumes content. Crowd voting comes in very handy when organizations deal with a large volume of data and need help in sifting through such data to make logical sense. This is becoming increasingly common these days where organizations are attempting to solve big data issues—big data is a rapidly growing discipline and works on the principles of data engines, analytics, and machine-based learning/unlearning to draw meaningful results from large data sets. While big data engineering is a growing and promising space, crowd voting comes in as a quick interim solution to invite the crowd to vote and help sort through the available data. Typical areas of use include reality shows on media and voting/poll contests on social networks (typically conducted by retail organizations). Results from these voting efforts are often used by the organization that initiated the survey or for whom the survey was conducted. The core motivators for the crowd to participate in such an effort include fun, brand loyalty, and community involvement. Money is usually not a driving force in crowd voting. The process is so simple that someone from the crowd can finish the voting process in as little as 5 minutes, and with the platforms available to enable the crowd to participate (be it their mobile devices or social networks), the input from the crowd comes in within very short periods of time. Even if an organization hires a group of experts to help it make the call on the question at hand, the results would not be as representative, as quick, and as accurate as to what the crowd provides. Some prevalent examples of crowd voting include the following:

American Idol, the popular reality singing show, has the crowd rating and voting for their favorite contestants. Similarly, threadless.com is another great example where the crowd votes on t-shirt designs to decide which ones go in to production. Pictorially speaking, here are some interesting examples from the beverage company Vitamin Water[34] and the apparel brand Limited (picture taken from one of the author's, Rajini's, Facebook profile) that we can relate to in our day-to-day world that belong to the crowd voting category (Figures 2.3 and 2.4).

Figure 2.3   Real-world voting and polling examples for crowd voting.

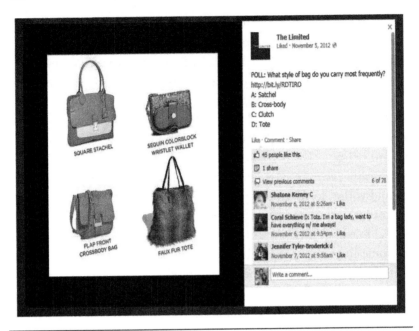

Figure 2.4 Real-world voting and polling examples for crowd voting.

Crowd Wisdom

The word *wisdom* is used a lot in the context of crowdsourcing. The message to bear in mind here is that the collective wisdom of the crowd yields very valuable input and is often very precise and close to accuracy. So, if we look at defining *crowd wisdom*, going by its name again, this is where the wisdom or know-how of the crowd is leveraged to solve problems. This technique has a very thin line of difference between the earlier one of crowd creation. Herein the crowd does not create content per se. It does provide tangible results, be it in terms of answers, defects in case of software testing, input, etc.; however, it does not create anything, unlike in the case of crowd creation. It provides answers to questions or provides feedback on something that has already been created. For example, in the reality show *Who Wants to Be a Millionaire?* of the set of lifelines available to the contestant (which are asking an expert, 50-50 choice, and asking the audience), asking the audience fetches the right answer 91% of the time compared to asking the expert, who is right 65% of the time.[10] While it is heartening to see that the wisdom of the crowd herein exceeds that of the expert, we are more interested in the crowd's collective wisdom, its precision, richness, and diversity, as opposed to comparing its outcomes with that of the experts' outcomes. As mentioned in this case, reality shows tend to be an area where crowd wisdom is relied upon a whole lot. Software quality assurance and testing, which is the focus of our book, also falls under this umbrella of crowd wisdom. Depending on what crowd wisdom is being used for, the crowd motivators could be money (e.g., in cases such as software testing), fun and community involvement (e.g., in cases such as reality shows), or a loyalty for a specific brand/product transparency. Exchange markets are also a powerful area where crowd wisdom is used. Herein, based on the crowd's reactions and input, the positioning and share price for a certain listing may go up or down. The results from a crowd wisdom exercise can be collectively used either by an organization or an individual, depending on what use and discipline the information is sought for. Pictorially speaking, the SIM exchange banner in Figure 2.5 shows how crowd wisdom is used in positioning video games and accordingly deciding best-seller positions.

The examples we discussed at the start of this book, on the ox weighing competition and the cereal counting competition, also fall under

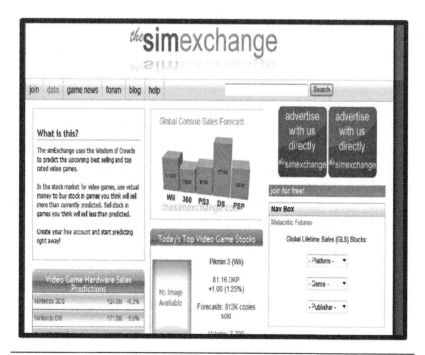

Figure 2.5   SIM exchange—a real-world example of crowd wisdom.[35]

the crowd wisdom category. The interesting point to note about crowd wisdom is that the time it takes to gather the wisdom can be alarmingly different from one task to another. This is from the standpoint of the crowd. Let us look at this from the varied forms that we have discussed so far. In the case of *crowd creation*, one can safely assume it will take a considerable amount of time given that new content is being created. Crowd voting can be assumed as one that hardly takes any time. However, crowd wisdom can be quite variant in the time it takes the crowd to complete the task, depending on the task at hand—for example, a software testing task may take quite some time, whereas a quick input such as in the case of a reality show or an ox weighing competition will hardly take a few minutes. Crowd wisdom is huge in its scope and will be the basis of our discussion in the subsequent chapters of this book. It might interest you to try some simple exercises with a chosen crowd at your end, to prove the case in point about its collective wisdom. If so, we suggest you take specific questions to the crowd—questions that are not very simple and at the same time not very complex in nature. Some examples could include: Which individual has won the most Oscars so far? On which country's flag do you see a serpent and an eagle? You can ask these as multiple choice questions or as open-ended questions. Or if you would like to take this further and prove an exercise statistically, you can try an exercise similar to the cereal counting one that we discussed earlier, in Chapter 1.

Crowd Funding

The last technique that we will look at under the crowdsourcing umbrella is crowd funding. This area, again, as the name goes, is one where the crowd funds specific projects. This is still an evolving area and probably one that is the least mature of the other crowdsourcing models.[11] The idea here is to have the crowd evaluate and fund projects that it believes in and wants to support. The foundation of this model has great potential and is very welcoming, as it supports projects, individuals, and entities that might otherwise be denied credit or opportunity, if the mainstream investing approach is adopted. Often projects of a compelling nature, be they in public welfare, healthcare, infrastructure, or economic and social improvement, are kick-started through crowdsourced funds. While this could be one extreme of it, on the other side, young entrepreneurs who have a promising idea also often use the crowd funding model to reach out to their friends, families, and community at large to pool funds. It need not just be an individual, but a group of individuals who are just starting off a company or bootstrapping a project that can also leverage the crowd funding model. Typically, the motivator for the crowd that funds the project is money where they get a good return on the investment they make. However, a more important motivator in this case is their drive for the common good, satisfaction from supporting a not-for-profit cause or giving an opportunity to a deserving entrepreneur. As mentioned earlier, this is a still an up-and-coming model, as there are quite some legal implications in raising money in public, especially when you are not a public company and are also raising funds spanning across geographies. The Obama administration signed the Crowd Funding JOBS (Jumpstart our Business Startups) Act in April 2012, easing the crowd funding process and empowering start-ups to raise funds in public, up to a certain amount, without being registered with the Securities and Exchange Commission (SEC).[12] The other well-known platform for crowd funding is Kickstarter, which empowers individuals to expose their projects and raise funds. Several such examples of crowd funding platforms are available online, and one interesting compilation of such domain-specific platforms to leverage is available on alumnifutures.com.[13]

Is Crowdsourcing the Same as Outsourcing?

Outsourcing has been in existence for quite some time now. Organizations have been outsourcing work to vendors for the last three decades or so. Industry now has a very mature set of processes and vendors of varying sizes and subject matter expertise, making outsourcing an established working model in the software development world. However, with the introduction of crowdsourcing, especially where some define crowdsourcing as *crowd + outsourcing*, there is a commonly lingering question as to whether crowdsourcing is the same as outsourcing. This is precisely why we wanted to have a separate section to discuss this topic. Having looked at what crowdsourcing is in our earlier sections of this chapter, let us look at a simple definition on what outsourcing is. Outsourcing, simply put, is contracting with a third-party organization or individual to get a specific job done with external resources instead of internal resources.

You can almost look at crowdsourcing and outsourcing to form a Venn diagram where there are some elements in common, while there are others that are unique to each of them, individually. More specifically, here is a noninvasive list of core points in common and in uniqueness:

In common:
1. Both involve getting work done from specific entities, outside of the core project team.
2. Both can be applied to organizations of varying scale, size, technology, and domain.
3. Both need the support of the core project team and the stakeholder team to succeed.

In uniqueness:
1. Crowdsourcing can be driven by motivators other than just money, whereas outsourcing is almost exclusively driven by money (except in cases of a free pilot where the vendor is trying to establish its worth to the prospective client).
2. Crowdsourcing can be done with internal employees of the organization (outside of the core project team), whereas outsourcing engages people external to the organization.
3. Crowdsourcing payment models can be quite unique in that you could pay the crowd tester per valid bug or on a time and materials basis. In outsourcing, typically payments are on time and materials or a fixed-bid basis (these days service level agreements are becoming more popular, where valid bugs' count could be one of the payment-deciding parameters).
4. In crowdsourcing typically you engage with individuals rather than with companies (although you have a few companies today that specialize in crowdsourced testing or offer crowdsourced testing as an add-on service in their portfolio). For example, we at QA InfoTech, although primarily an independent third-party testing services provider, are not just an outsourcing test vendor, but are also open to and have helped our clients with some crowdsourced testing solutions. On the contrary, in outsourcing, you typically work with companies and only in special scenarios engage with freelance outsourced consultants.

5. Crowdsourcing typically does not involve legal agreements except in certain specific scenarios, such as private betas where a binding nondisclosure agreement may be asked for. Outsourcing is bound by a legal agreement enforceable at law.

6. To reap the true value of a crowdsourced test effort, you try to maintain as much independence as possible between your crowd testers and also do not expose them to specific system internals as you want them testing from a pure end user standpoint. In outsourcing, as the team ramps up on the product, a healthy practice would be to encourage them to become an extended arm of the core team and provide them details of system internals to empower them to find as many defects as possible.

7. Specific areas such as test automation, build verification test execution, and regressions do not benefit much from crowdsourced testing given the lack of proven predictability from crowd testers (also bound by the fact that there is no legal binding with the crowd team). On the other hand, areas such as usability, accessibility, and realistic load testing using live users go a long way with a crowd team. This distinction is important to keep in mind in deciding areas where crowdsourced testing and outsourced testing would complement and supplement each other.

Based on this list, it is evident that crowdsourcing and outsourcing have more differences than similarities, and each brings its own value to the table. So, there is no denying which is superior over another; rather, it is important to understand how each project would benefit from both and plan an implementation strategy to maximize the project's return on investments.

What Is Crowdsourced Testing and Where Does It Fit in This Picture?

Earlier in this chapter, we saw how crowdsourced testing is a part of the crowd wisdom umbrella. Online resources are plentiful these days with professional and casual bloggers, authors and writers who share their knowledge on varied topics through formal definitions, examples, illustrations, podcasts, etc. Crowdsourcing and crowdsourced testing are limelight areas in the recent years with a lot of online discussion and definitions. While we will look at our own definition to understand crowdsourced testing in a simple and comprehensive manner, here are other popular definitions worth looking at:

Dailycrowdsource.com: "Crowd sourcing is the process of getting work, usually online, from a crowd of people. The word is a combination of the words '**crowd**' and '**outsourcing**'. The idea is to take work and outsource it to a crowd of workers."

In this above definition, the words *crowd* and *outsourcing* catch our attention, and as we have discussed in the previous section, we now understand the similarities and differences between these two terms in getting a holistic view on what crowdsourced testing is.

CrowdSourcing.org: "Welcome to the new world of crowd sourced testing, an emerging trend in software engineering that exploits the benefits, effectiveness, and efficiency of crowd sourcing and the **cloud platform** towards software quality assurance and control. With this new form of software testing, the product is put to test under **diverse platforms**, which makes it more **representative, reliable, cost-effective, fast,** and above all, **bug-free.**

We have again called out phrases/keywords that are important in this definition with a bold font. Involving the crowd in testing will definitely increase the product quality's reliability and make it more end user representative. It is also a great add-on solution when the team is operating within time and cost constraints. However, what we do not accept in this definition is the claim that the product now becomes bug-free. As testers, we all know that while we need to exercise due diligence, and represent end users in finding and eliminating defects as quickly and early as possible in an software development life cycle (SDLC), it is not possible to certify any product as bug-free. We sign off on a product based on objective parameters that we define as exit criteria, possibly with some known issues and with an understanding that there may be issues that the end user will report once the product is live.

Our goal in ensuring quality is to be able to deliver a product with rich functionality and of exceptional usability and performance that the end user can use in a secure manner. Once the product is live, the jury is out with the end users, who can even provide suggestions and recommendations to fix in subsequent releases, and the tester is no magician to eliminate all bugs 100% and foresee such suggestions in advance.

CrowdsourceTesting.com: "Crowd sourcing your software testing consists of **delegating** onto a number of internet users the task of testing your web or software project while in development to ensure that it contains no defects, referred to as bugs."

While this definition is fairly representative in understanding what crowdsourced testing is, we would herein prefer using the word *engaging* rather than *delegating*. As we discussed in the previous section in crowdsourcing, you typically engage to work with a crowd; you do not delegate work to them in most scenarios, as they form a free-flowing group of people who test your product like an end user would, to provide feedback. While you could delegate specific tasks on to them, you will realize that you reap the most success when you engage with the crowd rather than delegate to the crowd.

So, how can we define crowdsourced testing in simple phrases to help us understand the practical meaning in implementing it? Is it a model where you pay testers for valid bugs they find, like what most people think it is? While this is also crowdsourced testing, this is not the only manifestation it takes. Crowdsourced testing manifests itself in varied forms. Simply put, crowdsourced testing is *leveraging the community at large in testing your product and providing feedback.*

This process may or may not involve money, but it typically leverages the crowd for one or more of the following reasons:

1. **The crowd's testing know-how:** While an internal team is falling short on testing resources, the crowd could be used to address the team's spike needs or to supplement the internal team's testing efforts on an ongoing basis.
2. **The crowd's subject matter expertise (SME):** You may run into a scenario where your domain knowledge internal to the

team is limited or can be strengthened with an external source, in which case an SME-driven crowd would be a great addition to the team. For example, think of medical professors who could be testing your medical software and providing feedback.

3. **The crowd's end user representation:** While the tester typically represents the end user within the team, nothing can equate having a real end user use the product and give feedback. In the same example above, think of doctors, nurses, and medical practitioners using your medical software to give you real-time feedback. You may term this beta testing, dog fooding, etc., but the ultimate action involved in getting the end user to test your product is the act of crowdsourced testing.

While all three reasons listed above are strong enough to justify engaging with the crowd, there is more value in using them for their subject matter expertise and end user representation than for their testing know-how. You can always source testers internally, but these other two areas of end user representation and subject matter expertise are where it will be difficult and expensive to source internal testers. These are where there is the most bang for the buck in engaging with the crowd in your quality assurance activities.

Now, let's move on to talking about where crowdsourced testing fits under the crowdsourcing umbrella. Having looked at the varied forms of crowdsourcing, we now understand that crowdsourced testing takes a solid seat under the crowd wisdom umbrella, where we leverage the wisdom of the crowds to find issues and solve problems. There is a thin line of difference here as to whether software testing belongs to the crowd creation or crowd wisdom category. For example, if the crowd were to create test cases and test plans, would it not fall under the crowd creation category? While it is not impossible or uncommon to have the crowd create test cases, it is not a very valuable use of its time. The true value of the crowd in software quality assurance and testing is reaped when it plays with the product like how an end user would and provides its feedback. In this case, more than creation, it is the crowd's wisdom that we want to target to have it find defects (not create defects), which is why the crowd wisdom category wins in pulling software testing under its belt, over crowd creation.

Understanding Crowdsourced Testing through Examples

We said crowdsourced testing is as simple (yet powerful) as leveraging the community to test your product and provide feedback. What is the community here? What kind of testing can we engage it in? How do we build or reach out to the community? Obviously, these are very valid questions to be answered in successfully implementing crowdsourced testing. While we will focus on some of the implementation aspects in great detail in the next couple of chapters, here are simple examples on how crowdsourced testing can be flexibly adopted within a tester's testing environment.

1. Think of working with other employees in your organization outside of the core project team. As people who are not aware of the product or its system internals in detail, they are an excellent bunch of people to leverage as an internal crowd. You could leverage them for any of the reasons we discussed earlier—because of their testing experience, domain knowledge, or end user representation. For example, your application may be one that is to be used internally and they are the real users. Or you may be a building a mobile application that you need tested on a range of mobile devices and platforms, where it is difficult for you to have all of these devices in your mobile test lab. Extending the invite to others in your company expands your test coverage and excites the internal crowd as they get to see the cool and geeky applications the company is working on, making it a win-win scenario for everyone involved.

2. Explore building a beta team for your product and customizing it to meet your product's needs. For example, have a banker, banker's client (power users and regular users), administrator, bank shareholder, and bank executive as part of your beta crowd team if you are building a banking application. Having such a rich and diverse crowd supplement the test efforts of your internal team will go a long way in enriching your product's quality. This, however, is easier said than done. It takes time to build such a careful pool of crowd (that is, a trusted crowd) users to help you with your test efforts, so start early, engage continuously, and dedicate the required overhead to work with the crowd team.

3. Explore partnerships with organizations and universities to bring in the subject matter expertise or specific testing specialization that you may lack in-house. For example, if you are building a global application where the translated content is very important to be verified, think about reaching out to colleges that offer language courses in specific locales that you need your content to be verified in.

One can be very successful in a crowdsourced test effort if adequate time and thought are put into planning and implementing the effort diligently (Chapter 5 will completely focus on this topic); in addition, all it takes is to be creative and think out of the box on what constitutes the crowd and how you can build such a crowd to help in your specific project. As you can see, all the examples discussed above are not so difficult solutions to implement. One needs to just explore avenues with an open mind to leverage the crowd to test and benefit the project at hand.

In 1952, the American economist Harry Markowitz presented his modern portfolio selection theory, in which he talked about diversification of funds in a portfolio to reduce risks and maximize investments. If you look at a 401(k) investment portfolio as an example in the current-day world, this theory holds very true. This theory has a striking relationship with crowdsourced testing in that one can easily remember crowdsourced testing as the application of the portfolio selection theory in quality assurance. Pictorially, it can be remembered as seen in Figure 2.6, where one brings in a diverse crowd with an increased chance of getting diverse feedback to maximize returns and reduce risks.

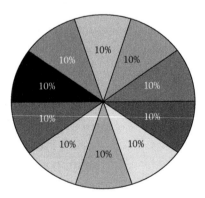

Figure 2.6 Crowdsourced testing: portfolio selection theory applied to quality assurance.

The Rising Popularity of Crowdsourcing

Although a concept/technique/model has been in place for several decades or centuries, it sometimes soars in popularity overnight. This is exactly what happened with crowdsourcing. We talked about how crowdsourcing in varied forms has existed since the 18th century, but it was Jeff Howe's article in 2006 that gave crowdsourcing the attention it deserved. Since then, there has been no looking back. Organizations as well as the general public have started using crowdsourcing in various forms. Interestingly, as we write this book, we were looking up to see whether we can include catchy slogans on crowdsourcing. As we searched for this, we stumbled on various crowdsourcing platforms where one can submit his or her requests to get catchy slogans on specific keywords. Organizations and the general public are now willingly reaching out to the crowd to obtain solutions to their problems and questions. While the concept can only attain a certain amount of popularity with the person who gave it due attention (Jeff Howe in this case), the rest needs to follow by merit of its own strengths, benefits, and value-add. That is exactly what has been happening with both crowdsourcing and crowdsourced testing. Organizations and people realize that, given the constraints they operate within (be it timelines, costs, or competition in the marketplace), crowdsourcing is an excellent solution (although often a supplemental solution and not a stand-alone solution) to leverage. Several success stories are out in the marketplace on how crowdsourcing is being used, which adds to the market confidence in the concept. Also, this is a model with a vast scope not limited by technology, domain, company scale, size, or type. This is another main reason for its being increasingly used in the last few years. Pictorially speaking, see Figure 2.7.

The other reason for this model to soar is the demand and supply factors at play. We will talk about this in greater detail in Chapter 3, but keep in mind that given the kinds of products that are being developed, end user expectations from products, and global technology penetration, a solution of this scale has become necessary to help the industry play catch-up in its software development and testing practices.

Finally, another very important reason for the rising popularity of crowdsourcing is the factor of empowerment. If the concept was introduced alone and the industry did not have facilitating

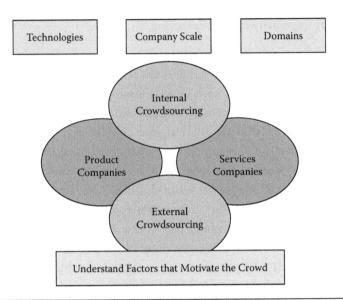

Figure 2.7   The breadth and depth of crowdsourcing.

technologies to leverage the crowd, the model would not have seen much light of day. The growth in social technologies and networks, cloud computing, increasing demand and supply for mobile computing, introduction of high-end devices, including mobile phones, tablets, and e-readers, and increasing use of agile practices that demand organizations to consider continuous and iterative development models have all necessitated and supported crowdsourcing and crowdsourced testing. All of these factors along with crowdsourcing form a very cohesive and cooperative chain in bringing the world together in global production and consumption of products and services. This is only a start, and the scope for crowdsourcing is only going to increase in the years to come, which we will briefly touch upon in Chapter 9.

Did You Know?[D-3,D-4]

Crowdsourcing is being used even in highly secure domains, such as banking and financial services. Examples include:

- Commonwealth Bank (Australia): Its crowdsourcing project IdeaBank enables clients to post, vote, and discuss ideas on new innovative products and services.

- HSBC (USA): Considered to be the first bank to crowdsource, HSBC launched the first direct lab. The bank now directly collaborates with its customers, sharing feedback, creating new products, as well as enhancing existing services.
- Danske Idebank (Denmark): It had a crowdsourcing initiative called Idebank. The goal was to demonstrate its willingness to be a different bank, involving the Danish population in its transformation. At the end of the first version of this program Danske Bank had 263 ideas, 185 comments, and 3109 votes.
- NyKredit Saving Tips (Denmark): It crowdsourced an initiative called Sparetips. In just 2 months it gathered 400 tips that were 100% user generated, without any reward strategy or contest.
- Deutsche Bank Drive DB (Germany): It drove a crowdsourcing project, Drive DB, that involved corporate clients.
- DBS Bank (Singapore): It drove a crowdsourcing project, Your Bank—Your Design, on Facebook with the aim to create a branch design for generation Y clients.
- Barclays Bank (UK): It started an initiative, Barclaycard Ring card, to have its cardholders vote on card features.

Here are some examples of crowdsourcing taken up by big brands from across domains:

Nissan: drove a mareketing campaign asking users on social media to contribute ideas for the kind of technology to be incorporated in their cars

Citroen: launched a facebook application inviting users to choose the design for a special edition of the company's new C1 city car the C1 Connexion

Boehringer Ingelheim: a pharmaceutical company, relied on the wisdom of the scientific community, to design a model to predict the biological response of molecules, setting aside a $20,000 prize pool to be shared amongst contributors

Levi's: ran a crowdsourcing campaign on instagram getting 3500+ photo entries. The winner was staged in the 2012 "Go Forth" ad campaign

Expedia: ran a crowdsourced deals feature to share best deals from other travellers to its users. Although the crowd did not share this information, since it was created by the crowd, it was considered a form of crowdsourcing

Greggs: the bakery chain asked people on Facebook and Twitter to generate ideas for a festive song during the holiday season

Bobbi Brown: a cosmetics brand, ran a facebook campaign asking its 250,000 fans to vote for the lip color to bring back into production

3

WHY LEVERAGE THE CROWD FOR SOFTWARE TESTING?

Are You Ready to Stand Out in a Crowd?

Who would not want to stand out in a crowd? While this is an age-old idiom in use even today, if we apply this to software testing, crowdsourced testing holds excellent potential to help individuals who test the software (be they testers, budding testers, end users, or domain experts) bring out their best to not just strengthen the quality of the product under test, but also empower it to rise and stand out in a crowd. Why is this the case and why is crowdsourcing particularly relevant to software testing in the current times? This is what we will look at in detail in this chapter. To start looking at this, let us first understand where quality stands as of today.

A Peek at Software Quality

While it is not the goal of this book to introduce you to what software quality is, we will definitely take a quick look at it, to ensure we all have the same baseline to start with. Traditionally, the test team has always been responsible for software quality. They own software quality control and assurance, putting themselves in both a reactive and a proactive mode in ensuring the product is of exceptional quality in meeting and exceeding end user needs in the marketplace. While this rule of thumb has not changed and will not change, what is heartening to see in recent years is how quality is becoming a collective ownership. The product team as a whole is playing a role in its own space in possible ways in enhancing the quality of the product and the overall developmental effort. The test team still has its neck on the line for any missed issue/defect, but the product team as a whole is stepping in to analyze the issue objectively. With the active use of agile developmental models in a large number of organizations, such collective ownership of product quality is becoming inevitable. This is also helping push quality upstream, where the test team is empowering other teams to understand and implement quality in varied ways. For example, the tester can work with the:

- Development team in defining unit tests and giving them a set of automated tests to be run as part of their local testing efforts
- Build team in empowering them to run a set of build verification tests to ensure a build is test ready as soon as it is deployed
- Business team in incorporating end user scenarios into the product design, based on end user feedback and competitive analysis
- Operations and support team in analyzing issues from the field before they reach the triage team, filtering out any false alarms

Such proactive steps help the tester improve his own role as he is strengthening the quality of not just the product, but also the team's efforts and morale. This saves time for everyone and also helps the tester focus on more critical and value-added activities in product quality, such as competitor product analysis, static code reviews, code coverage analysis, exploratory testing, bug bashes, etc., for which he may not have had time otherwise.

Quality as a word often has an overloaded meaning. If one starts looking at its definition, there are varied versions of it, including definitions given by gurus in software testing. There are plenty of such definitions available online for reference. At a very simplistic level you can look at it as ensuring conformance to end user requirements in building a product that is scalable, secure, and usable. While several other parameters, such as schedule, time, cost, and feature set, play a role in the software development life cycle, quality tends to be the parameter that the product team attempts to dial up or down to keep the other parameters within defined levels. This is where the tester is an important torchbearer in ensuring quality is not compromised in this power struggle and that collectively the team gives objective importance to all parameters at play (Figure 3.1).

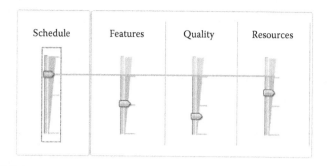

Figure 3.1 Parameters at play in a software development life cycle.

Software Quality in the Current Day and Age

In the earlier section, we looked at how software quality has become a collective ownership, with individual teams doing their bit in upholding the quality of both the product and their efforts. This is a welcoming change in recent years, and in continuation with this, there are other changes in the software quality landscape that we need to understand. Time to market is shrinking by the day. Driven by both the demanding end user wants and increasing competition in the marketplace, faster time to market has become one of the driving factors in determining an organization's success. Similarly, there is a close scrutiny on every dollar spent on the product, and the test effort is no exception. Every testing dollar spent is also looked at closely to understand and justify the return on investment.

Testing as a discipline has an elevated responsibility where a tester just cannot test against provided requirements and sign off on his task set. A tester is forced to look at the domain specifics of the product to understand the varied workflows and see what quality requirements they entail. For example, if you are testing a banking software, you need to understand workflows from varied user standpoints, banking regulations, mandates by the state and national governments, etc., in determining overall quality. While the product team as a whole will step in to meet the requirements from a domain standpoint, the tester is no exception and cannot continue to survive with just his core testing skills. Building subject matter expertise in the specific domain is becoming inevitable.

The tester also needs to understand what competition brings to the table in terms of functionality and performance to gauge how the product at hand is faring against them in making suitable recommendations internally. Although business teams are specifically tasked with this responsibility, this is an important step that the tester can take to differentiate himself from other testers and build a niche for himself.

On the marketplace front, the tester is being required to look at end user product consumption and usage patterns, and determine an optimized testing matrix, especially taking into account the multitude of mobile devices that the product/application is being used on these days. The compatibility matrix is far beyond the operating system and browser support of yesteryear. Mobile phones, tablets, and e-readers have all become very common form factors in accessing and using an application, forcing the tester to be on top of such usage patterns and determine the priority of the testing matrix along with what tests need to be run on each of them to ensure test coverage within the time and cost constraints on hand. Similarly, global releases of products and applications have become so common that the tester has to continue to focus on globalization and localization testing in building a happy customer base across geographies.

In the context of global releases, let us consider an advertisement (ad) campaign for better understanding of the issue at hand. Let us say a beverage is being launched globally and an ad campaign needs to be created for it. The marketing team herein needs to take into account the geographies the campaign will be launched in and whether the list includes any market that reads right to left. If so, the campaign with a sequence of images that reads left to right would send a completely opposite message, making it an anticampaign for the brand. While there are individual teams, such as the marketing teams in this case, that are chartered with these responsibilities, a tester who is an end user advocate needs to account for all these global forces at play in his test execution effort. See Figure 3.2.

With all of these factors at play, the challenges that a tester faces on the job are quite considerable. However, if you look at these as opportunities instead of challenges and as a natural evolution in the software development and testing discipline, you will start looking at the traditional software process holistically and see what can be done, what alternate and supplemental solutions can be brought in to tackle these challenges, build on these opportunities, and also maintain a tester's sanity.

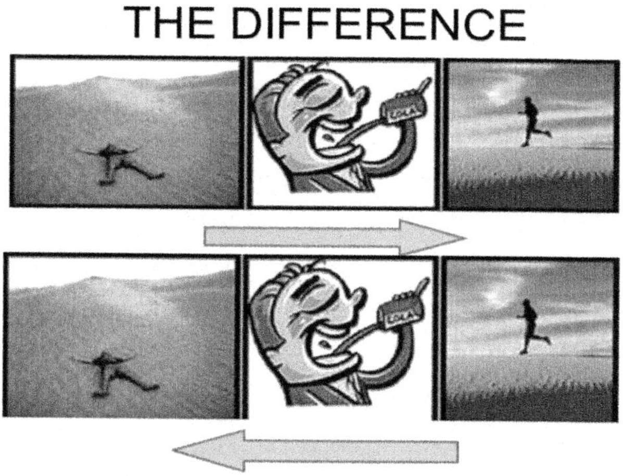

THE DIFFERENCE

Figure 3.2 A global ad campaign.[36]

The Need for Alternate Solutions to Assure and Control Software Quality

The traditional engagement models adopted in software quality assurance and control primarily revolve around insourced and outsourced testing. Insourced quality assurance (QA) is typically made up of a core QA team that is part of the larger product organization that directly employs them. Such an insourced team could also include contractors that are hired to directly work near or in the organization's premises. An outsourced team could be positioned on-site at the product company, nearshore at the vendor's premises, or offshore (be it at the product company's offshore offices or the vendor's premises). The insourced or outsourced team could also be deployed to work on the field as and when required. These engagement models that have long existed continue to be robust, but are they foolproof given the current need is the question we need to answer. With the changing needs of quality that we discussed in the previous section, a supplemental and newer solution is becoming inevitable. Such a solution needs to address or at least partially address the current needs where, along with the existing traditional solutions, it provides a foolproof answer to today's quality requirements. This is a solution that needs to:

- Bring in enhanced productivity to address the time constraints
- Provide coverage for end user devices and scenarios testing in realistic environments

- Be cost-efficient
- Account for the subject matter expertise or domain knowledge that the product needs and fill any internal gaps that the team may face
- Rope in real end users wherever possible in testing the product
- Provide an opportunity to create diversity in the quality efforts such that representative product feedback can be obtained

Do we have such a solution as of today? Is it being universally used and is it mature enough? Do all organizations know about such a solution? Is the solution being rightly implemented wherever it is used?

As a curious reader, you may have several such questions, and the simple answer to all of these is crowdsourced testing.

Tying the Gap in Quality to the Definition of Crowdsourced Testing

If we tie back the points in the last two sections to our earlier definition of crowdsourced testing, you will see the alignment evolve. You will see that crowdsourced testing is a supplemental, newer solution that has been evolving yet maturing over the last years, since Jeff Howe coined its name in 2006. This is the solution that will help organizations address their needs around enhanced productivity, faster time to market, lower costs, stronger subject matter expertise, and greater diversity in accounting for end user feedback in product testing. While all of these requirements align well with the solution on hand, it is important to understand that crowdsourced testing is not a stand-alone solution. It is and will continue to remain a supplemental solution—a solution that is leveraged in addition to the core testing team and outsourced testing team's efforts. Also, while the general market's direction around product development and software quality is what we are discussing, there are situations where it will not make sense to crowdsource your testing effort. We will talk about this in detail in Chapter 4; at this stage, you will mainly need to understand that crowdsourced testing is an effective supplemental solution to the traditional test engagement models, and it typically succeeds when the product has a large customer base that is globally spread, requires strong domain knowledge that is difficult to source and retain internally, and needs to be tested on a complex end user matrix that cannot be maintained in-house. Given all these requirements, and our earlier discussion point that crowdsourced testers can be brought in for their testing, domain/ subject matter expertise, or end user representation, you will see that crowdsourced testing is a perfect match for the current day's quality needs.

A Case Study on Facebook Relevant in the World of Agile Operations[C-1]

Over the course of this book, you will see in several places that one of the main reasons crowdsourced testing has gained prominence in recent years is the growth of social networking platforms that have greatly helped connect the crowd with the crowd seekers (organizations that want to leverage crowdsourced testing). While Facebook has tremendously helped in fostering crowdsourcing and crowd-sourced testing through various surveys, polls, and audience connections that organizations have been empowered with, it is also an interesting case study for us to look at as to why crowdsourced testing has become a true need of the current day supporting organizational agility all round. Even as we start discussing the case study, we will extend a disclaimer that Facebook does not have a formal QA team for its testing efforts. As an independent QA and testing services provider, we do not concur with this stand, but we respect Facebook's decision in line with its circumstances. Also, this is a point that is beyond the scope of our discussion for our current book, where we will only stick to how Facebook is leveraging the crowd for its testing and why such scenarios are noteworthy for other organizations too in the current day of agile operations.

Scenario

Facebook operates in a perpetual development mode. It has specific code releases (that require additional monitoring and testing) that happen weekly, while most releases happen twice a day. If we look at the software industry at large, the development timelines of organizations fall into one of the buckets shown in Table 3.1.

Table 3.1   Software Development Timelines

WATERFALL OR UNIFIED PROCESS	EVOLUTIONARY DEVELOPMENT	AGILE DEVELOPMENT	FACEBOOK	CONTINUOUS DEPLOYMENT
Once	Months	Weeks	One day	Less than an hour

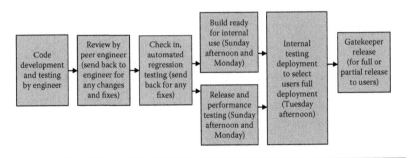

Figure 3.3   Facebook deployment cycle.

Given that pushes to production are happening at Facebook so frequently (which is quite typical in several other organizations too), if you look at the reasons for such rapid deployments, they can belong to one of the following categories: production fixes, major fixes, visible fixes, internal launches, product launches, user tests, etc.

Their release cycle in detail is as depicted in Figure 3.3.

Challenges Posed by Scale

Facebook's scale has increased manyfold ever since its inception. The front end undergoes continous development by hundreds of software engineers, committing code changes up to 500 times a day in about 3000 files. The code base size has reached around 10 million lines of code (LoC) in just about seven years of its existence. More than 1 billion users are logging into Facebook at least once monthly to connect and share content. Users are uploading upward of 2.5 billion content items every day. This level of activity is mind-boggling, and unless it has a development process (including testing) that matches it, scaling is going to be extremely difficult, if not impossible. While Facebook's scale may be unique to it, given its popularity and established presence in the marketplace, other organizations are possibly in a similar, if not the same, boat, where, in the agile world, they are dealing with several changes frequently, interacting with customers on a much more regular basis, and leveraging their speed in operations and performance as some of the core characteristics to outlive tight competition. Amid all of these, they do fully understand that quality cannot be compromised because just speed and performance will get them only so far. This is where a solution such as crowdsourced testing is very valuable. Again, while we reiterate that Facebook still does not have a formal QA team and we may not be in agreement with that, we respect its decision of working with the crowd in testing its product, which is why we have taken it as a case study for scenarios representative of what other organizations may also face today in a world where online services, direct interaction with the users, and an agile style of operations have all become so very inevitable.

Solutioning

Specific to the scale we discussed above and its situation, we will purely look at how Facebook is using the crowd. In our earlier definitions of crowdsourced testing, we talked about how it could potentially manifest itself in ways such as leveraging internal employees to test (those that are outside the core project), partnering with organizations for their subject matter expertise, and bringing in end users or representative end users to test, among some of the more valuable forms. Facebook has been leveraging most of these. It has two sets of releases going out weekly: one, which is a weekly release, for the more secure ones that need additional reviews and testing, starting on Sunday afternoons and hitting live by Tuesday, and the other, which are daily releases (even up to twice daily). In all of these, there is something called a default build that is released, which is a build thrown open to all Facebook employees (aka the internal crowd) involving them to test for the latest updates. In addition to this, when the build is released to the user base, there is something called a gatekeeper option, allowing the developer to decide the user base that gets to see the updates. So, this is almost like a private beta or a selective beta that goes out to specific users. The developer can decide based on various characteristics such as the user's geography, profile, etc., as to which categories of the user base should see the updates first, before they are thrown open to all of them. Once Facebook is comfortable, it throws open the updates to the full user base, and even at that point, it seeks feedback from them and actively monitors their activity through user logs and reports to understand how the changes are faring. Facebook also leverages its partners to test for all their updates and provide feedback. So, it is clearly leveraging crowdsourced testing in all possible ways to help ensure quality, especially when working in a mode of perpetual development, and this is a great case for organizations to understand and emulate in an agile world, helping them further augment their internal quality efforts.

Summary

According to the publication that we have referred to for this case study, some of the core summary points that are good takeaways for all of us include:

- Engineers have firsthand experience in the domain, but also need to test innovations on real users to see what works.
- Testing on real users at scale is possible, and provides the most precise and immediate feedback.

Leveraging Crowdsourced Testing in Various Testing Areas

As we begin to understand more about crowdsourced testing and where it would be relevant and valuable, we will dedicate one chapter on crowdsourced testing implementation practices (Chapter 5). Herein we will look at how to go about successfully planning and implementing a crowdsourced test effort. In the meantime, as a precursor, in this section let us see how crowdsourced testing can be leveraged for various testing areas, primarily from a manual testing angle.

Functional Testing

While this is the main area of focus in a product testing effort and is owned by the internal test team, the crowd can be of marginal value in testing a product from a functional standpoint. It would be ideal to engage it to play around the product's functionality from an exploratory angle rather than a guided and scripted angle based off of requirements. It can provide valuable feedback from a product's end-to-end functionality rather than focusing on module level functionality, which is best taken care of internally. One cannot go wrong in leveraging the crowd to test for functionality, whether it is brought in from the start of the product life cycle or at a later stage. Several teams engage with beta testers that form part of a larger crowd they use to provide feedback right from the design and planning stages given their subject matter expertise and past usage experience, in which case, they are able to give functional feedback even at a granular level.

UI Testing

User interface (UI) is a high return area when it comes to engaging the crowd. The crowd, especially an end user base-representing crowd, can provide strong UI feedback that aligns with its preferences. Since it aligns with the crowd's preferences and touches a softer and intangible aspect of the end user, the crowd can potentially add more value in UI testing than even the internal test team. And since UI is an area of focus primarily for end user facing pages, screens, and sections, this is an area where the crowd adds very high value through its tests and feedback. Domain expertise is very important in this case, compared to the crowd's end user representation.

Usability Testing

Usability again is a very subjective area, which touches the softer aspects of the end user. Is the application usable enough? Is it intuitive enough? While the core test team can adequately test for whether the application is usable and intuitive, the crowd can effectively answer whether the usability and intuitiveness factors are sufficient. Engaging the crowd to provide usability feedback, especially when the application is reasonably ready for end-to-end consumption, is definitely a smart move. Here the crowd's end user representation and domain expertise will be very handy. Since the usability factor largely depends on the domain understanding, this is one test area where subject matter expertise matters more than any other test area. For example, a doctor using a medical application would be able to provide much more realistic usability feedback than a regular crowd tester with no medical experience.

Accessibility Testing

This is yet another area where the crowd can add a lot of value since end user representation is very important here. However, this is a very selected crowd—a crowd with strong accessibility testing experience or a crowd that is more importantly challenged, be it physical, mental, or cognitive disabilities. In recent years, accessibility has been gaining a lot of stronghold, with governments mandating accessibility requirements to build products that are accessible by one and all. Section 508 in the United States and DDA in the UK are examples of compulsory accessibility standards that are being introduced globally. While accessibility experts can test a product/application using checklists developed to confirm adherence to these standards, none of these test efforts can match the additional value a challenged person can bring to the table using assistive technologies and tools such as screen readers, magnifiers, captioning tools, etc. Also, typically such challenged users are able to report not just defects in the current system, but also suggestions for future enhancements.

Performance Testing

This is an area that is given a lot of attention and focus in a test strategy in parallel to the core functional aspects. Typically, there is a separate team that focuses on performance testing the application from various angles, including load, stress, capacity and scalability, long haul, competitive baselining, etc. While the crowd cannot partake in all activities of performance testing due to infrastructure and system access limitations, if the product company diligently plans on how to use the crowd in this space, it can get some very valuable real-time feedback on the application's performance, which only the crowd can provide while still in the QA phase. Imagine having 10,000 live users from the crowd, from different geographies, infrastructure variables, and Internet bandwidth accessing the application in real time.

This is something that the internal team can never achieve even with the most sophisticated test environments to simulate the load. Similarly, page load and request response times on specific end user devices in their real-time usage environments are also very useful feedback areas to gain input on. While the crowd can add a lot of value here, it is important to understand when to engage the crowd in performance testing. In the ideal scenario the internal team would have conducted one round of performance tests to baseline the application's results before engaging the crowd, so as to minimize randomization and potential false alarms. Not much testing or domain expertise is required in providing performance feedback. Testing knowledge may come in handy; however, a basic application user with reasonable understanding of an application's performance and testing aptitude can be a good crowd tester in this space.

Security Testing

This test area derives marginal value from crowd testing. Security testing is a specialized area of focus even for the internal team and can turn out to be a very technical area to be handled by the crowd. A regular end user can provide some value here, especially around areas of authentication and authorization. However, you cannot expect the end user to focus on aspects such as spoofing, tampering with data, repudiation, attempting denial of service attacks, etc. A strong tester from the crowd community may be able to add value here, but this is one area where there is better value from the internal core testing team rather than the crowd. That said, programs such as "bug bounties"[14] are becoming popular by the day, where organizations such as Facebook leverage this technique to invite the crowd to test their application from a security angle and provide feedback. Bug bounty programs are often an open call to the public and a good manifestation of crowdsourced testing.

Globalization Testing

This is a high-value area as far as leveraging the crowd goes. Globalization is a very large space encompassing tests around internationalization, pseudolocalization, and localization. Localization is in itself a space of its own, covering localization functionality, UI, and translation. Since globalization heavily focuses on getting the application ready for global consumption and adapting to specific locales, a global crowd, be it a tester community or an end user (who primarily has the language expertise), can be of tremendous value here. This is especially the case when the application is launched in very specific locales that are not very commonly used and for which finding testers is not easy. Crowd testers herein not only provide functional and UI feedback in specific locales, but more importantly, provide translation assistance in confirming the suitability of the translated content for the market under discussion. LiveMocha is a great example of a language learning content and platform provider that leverages the crowd for both creating translated content and verifying it.

Compatibility Testing

Finally, touching on compatibility testing, this is yet another high-value area where the crowd can add a lot of value. Compatibility testing has lately become very challenging given the complex matrices that applications need to be tested on. Gone are the days where compatibility testing was restricted to just a simple operating system and browser set. Devices that users access the application on are growing by the day, with the mobile revolution that the market has been facing in the last decade. Smartphones, e-readers, tablets, and laptops, along with their corresponding OS and browser versions, are mind-boggling to account for, especially within the tight timeline and cost constraints the teams operate within. However, compatibility testing cannot be compromised—a fully functional and performing application that fails on compatibility will definitely lose market share very soon. In defense of the test team, it is not possible to stock all devices in-house given the expense and difficulty in procuring them. Further, they may soon become obsolete, bringing down the overall return on investment in purchasing such devices for testing purposes. With all of these in mind, if you turn to the crowd, you will see tremendous value in bringing in a crowd (be it testers, domain experts, or end users) that possesses such devices and can readily use them for short-term testing needs. In addition to that, since end users test for compatibility in their realistic environments, the overall value of leveraging the crowd for compatibility testing cannot be ignored or emphasized enough.

In this section, we talked about various test areas and how some of them are high-value zones in bringing in the crowd and some yield marginal value. The product team, more specifically, the test team, has to make its call on which areas to leverage the crowd for, specific to the project's needs, such that the value is maximized and the risk (which we will see in greater detail in Chapter 4) is minimized. With all of this discussion in place, while you would appreciate the value the crowd brings in, in enhancing software quality, you will also need to account for the model's challenges and limitations to get a holistic view into what it offers to your project at hand. Even for your own testing environment, the crowd's value may differ from one project to another, so understanding that this is a very custom solution every time you use it is a key to succeeding in a crowdsourced testing engagement, which is what we will focus on in the rest of this book.

Did You Know?[D-5]

Having talked about the definitions of *crowdsourcing* and specifically *crowd wisdom*, let's take a quick look at comparing and contrasting group brainstorming versus crowdsourcing:

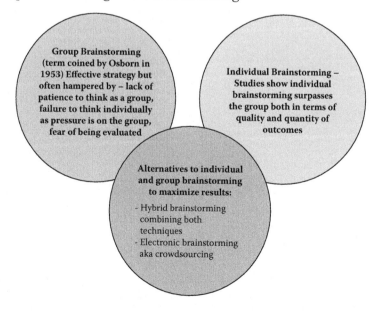

Group Brainstorming (term coined by Osborn in 1953) Effective strategy but often hampered by – lack of patience to think as a group, failure to think individually as pressure is on the group, fear of being evaluated

Individual Brainstorming – Studies show individual brainstorming surpasses the group both in terms of quality and quantity of outcomes

Alternatives to individual and group brainstorming to maximize results:
- Hybrid brainstorming combining both techniques
- Electronic brainstorming aka crowdsourcing

4

Is Crowdsourced Testing a No-Brainer Solution to All Quality Problems?

Practice doesn't make perfect. Practice reduces the imperfection.

—**Toba Beta**
Master of Stupidity[37]

No solution is a perfect solution that works in all scenarios and at all times. Some solutions just cannot be applied in certain scenarios, while others need to be customized and applied with care to maximize benefits and minimize risks. Crowdsourced testing also sails the same boat and is no exception to this statement that no solution is perfect, despite all the strong benefits of this model that we have been talking about. As in any situation, it is important to understand the problem statement, the potential solutions, and weigh the pros and cons of each solution before deciding the best approach to take. Also, it is important to practice the solution—try it in smaller chunks before going in for a large crowdsourced test effort so you have prior learning specific to your needs that you can take into account in building a crowdsourced testing strategy. In this chapter we will start looking at when crowdsourced testing does not work. Understanding this is even more important than understanding when it will work. We will then look at the challenges and limitations of this model to help understand if it is a solution worth pursuing for your specific needs. A view into the challenges and limitations will help you build a mitigation and optimization strategy to maximize your return on investment from crowdsourced testing.

As a precursor, let us look at *when crowdsourced testing succeeds.* This will help you map your needs to see if crowdsourced testing is really what you need.

While the crowd can bring in value of varying degrees, once you have put together a team, it brings in the most value when the team is diverse in nature. For example, if you are building a social application, you would greatly benefit from a diverse crowd that spans across age groups, geographies, educational background, cultural and economic diversity, etc., as opposed to having a crowd that is homogeneous. Heterogeneity is a key to deriving the most from a crowd testing effort, especially when the diversity is what best represents your live end user base. When such diversity is brought in, oftentimes it is not possible to have a tightly coupled communication link between your crowd testers, and incidentally, this is good for your project. As far as possible, maintain independence among your crowd testers, as that is when you can have them bring out their best in testing your product and providing feedback. There may be specific situations, especially in cases such as closed beta groups, where you may let your crowd testers talk to each other through email distribution lists, conference calls, etc. This is a judicious decision you make based on your project's time and complexity factors where knowledge sharing among the crowd will help bring down the overall overhead in managing the team, especially in products that are technically very complex to test. In such cases, it makes sense to introduce the crowd members to one another, whereas in most other cases the crowd succeeds when there is independence. Imagine a scenario where I build an e-commerce site and I bring in the crowd to test it. Why would I want crowd tester A to know what scenarios crowd tester B tried? This just adds to the communication overhead and, more importantly, impedes into tester A's creativity in testing my product.

Take time to understand if your product is going to benefit from end user feedback or is in a complex domain where it is difficult or expensive for you to source and retain domain experts within your company. Such cases are great candidates to bring in the crowd where you are setting them up for success. For example, let's say I am building a language software to teach people specific languages. I have the content created and verified by a team of internal experts, but I am looking at bringing in the crowd (native language speakers) to verify the content. This is a great scenario to bring in the crowd, as it is not practically feasible, from sourcing and expense standpoints, to hire testers with the language knowledge and keep them on the team. Similarly, when end user scenarios are difficult and impractical to simulate in-house, bringing in the crowd is a very successful option to leverage. Let us take the example of having to test an application across a range of mobile devices. While several simulator options are available these days, specific tests, especially around device-specific compatibility and performance taking into account the device's form factor, are realistic only when tested with a physical device in live end user environments such as Internet bandwidth. It is not a practical solution to source and build a mobile test lab with all the needed devices. This is a classic case where building a crowd team that is able to test on real end user environments is a proven path to success.

Finally, an important factor to ensuring the crowd's success is to identify tasks where you will benefit and also be able to align with the crowd's motivating factors. If you are able to identify such a magic mix to satisfy your and the crowd's needs, you are well on your path to succeeding in your crowd testing implementation. We will discuss this, along with specific examples, in greater detail in Chapter 5.

What Not to Crowdsource in Your Test Effort

When to apply a solution to a problem is one thing to know. But the more critical piece is when not to apply a solution to a problem, as failing to see this can have a much more detrimental effect than not applying the solution at all. The adverse impact may even outweigh the positives that a right solution can bring to the problem. Given the importance of this topic, we discuss this even before looking at what to crowdsource in your testing effort. When looking at what not to crowdsource in your test effort, you will have to analyze scenarios from various standpoints, such as:

- Value-add the solution brings to the table from quality, time, and cost angles
- Test team and product team morale
- Stakeholder buy-in

Do not crowdsource areas or features that have a lot of moving pieces and are very dynamic in nature: Such tasks may make the communication process very cumbersome and pull down the team's morale (both the crowd testers and the internal team that is working with the crowd). For example, let's say in the application you are developing you have integration points that are impending from other groups in your organization or from external vendors where traction has been difficult to obtain. If the internal team is itself struggling to get a handle of such pieces of work, the randomization is only going to further increase by bringing in the crowd. In fact, this may just be timing issue, where after some time the dust might settle and the external dependencies would have greatly reduced. It may help to bring in the crowd at such a time.

Do not crowdsource if your intellectual property (IP) is very sensitive: Clearly every product or application that is being built is the organization's IP. It would want to hold it high from varied angles, be it establishing itself as a leader in the marketplace, from legal and competitive angles, leveraging it to provide value-add to its clients, etc. Given the need to safeguard one's IP, typically in scenarios where the product's IP is very sensitive or you need to work in a stealth mode, the organization needs to be very wary of using a crowd test team. Unless you have a very controlled crowd test team (sometimes referred to as a trusted crowd) in place, it will become very difficult to validate your crowd's identity—for example, a crowd tester could very well even be a competitor of yours wanting to understand your feature set and implementation details. So, make a call if your IP is highly sensitive and needs to be in stealth at certain stages in your software development life cycle or, for that matter, even throughout the release cycle to determine whether or not you should take the crowd testing route.

Environment-specific complexity: We discussed earlier that in complex end user environments, it is very valuable to leverage a crowd test team. On the flip side, if the test environment is very complex and cannot be scaled yet for the crowd's access, then it does not make sense to crowd test your effort, at least for the time being, until such complexities are ironed out.

Tasks that require regular turnaround: Testing tasks are often quite diverse in nature in terms of their size, complexity, and frequency. Some tasks are specifically very frequent and recurring in nature, such as build verification tests that are run even on a daily basis based on the build release frequency.

These are tasks that are formal and need a regular turnaround from the test team and, in fact, areas where the test team needs to closely collaborate with the development and the build/operations teams. For such tasks, bringing in the crowd would be a total mismatch adversely affecting the overall value-add and the morale of everyone involved.

Core testing tasks: Again, going by what we discussed in the previous point, some testing tasks are very formal and recurring in nature. Some are very core to the overall testing process and integrate so tightly with the product and the core team that it would not be wise to loosely couple them from the core effort so as to use the crowd in testing them. These tasks, for example, test automation, initial performance, security and integration baselining, test-driven development work, core regression test pass execution, etc., are best retained internally (whether with the core team or the outsourced team) from return on investment (ROI) and team morale standpoints. On a slightly different note, tasks that are mundane in nature and that do not require a lot of diversity from the crowd are also best retained internally to avoid the overhead of working with a crowd test team. For example, running a regression test pass (not regressing specific bugs, but running a full suite of planned regression tests, whether manually or through automation) is best done by the internal team.

As we look at what not to crowdsource in your test effort, here's a live example worth considering. This is a study that was conducted by the University of Texas, Austin, for a usability test that it conducted with both an internal team and an external crowd usability team. This was a university website that it wanted testing to be done on and for which it brought in the two teams for their usability studies. The outcome of the study is shown in Table 4.1.

The similarities and differences in the issues identified by the two groups are as seen in Table 4.2. Given that the internal usability test team comprised ongoing users of the website, it was able to find more complex issues, such as invisible tools, missing links, etc., while the crowd usability team found more intuitiveness-related issues, such as unclear navigation and difficulty in finding specific features such as search.

Table 4.1 In-House vs. External Crowd Usability Testing: Premise

	LAB USABILITY TEST	CROWDSOURCED USABILITY TEST
Participants	5	55 (of which 14 were later found to be spammers)
Participant demographics	Students	Crowd workers
Age range	24–33	19–51
Education level	Bachelor's degree and master's degree	All levels
Experience with similar websites	Yes: 100%	Yes: 77% No: 23%
Speed	Approximately 30 minutes per session	Less than 4 hours total
Participant costs	None	$2.92 for pilot tests $23.41 for final tests (Average: $0.48/tester)

Table 4.2 In-House vs. External Crowd Usability Testing: Results

MAJOR PROBLEMS IDENTIFIED	LAB USABILITY TEST	CROWDSOURCING USABILITY TEST
Font size too small	×	×
Out-of-date information	×	×
Menu overlap	×	×
Irrelevant picture	×	×
Invisible tools	×	
Information not cross-linked	×	
Lack of sort function	×	
Navigation unclear		×
Search box difficult to locate		×

Table 4.3 Pros and Cons of External Crowd Usability Testing

ADVANTAGES	DISADVANTAGES
More participants	Lower-quality feedback
High speed	Less interaction
Low cost	Spammers
Various backgrounds	Less focused user groups

If you analyze the pros and cons of using an external crowd team in this situation, you can easily come up with a list like that shown in Table 4.3.

As takeaways from this study,[15] both teams added value in their own ways. In fact, in this specific example, the internal team was also a classic crowd candidate, where we have discussed earlier that you can also leverage an internal team for your crowdsourced test effort. However, one thing to keep in mind is that in this usability study, the kind of questions asked need to be a customized list specific to the group of people. You cannot use the same questions for the internal and the external crowd because the levels of know-how about the product/application are different in both cases. The customization will help you leverage that know-how and get specific feedback, thus increasing your overall test coverage and results.

Challenges and Limitations of a Crowdsourced Test Effort

Looking at areas where crowdsourced testing might not work is one thing. Given that crowdsourced testing is largely applicable in a wide range of other areas, as seen in earlier chapters, one must recognize the challenges and limitations of the model. Understanding these and working on an approach that will mitigate them will go a long way in implementing a successful crowdsourced test effort. Such due diligence on the part of the team that takes on crowdsourced testing will also serve as a precedence to other groups in an organization, help win stakeholder approval much faster, and increase overall internal confidence in the test effort.

Most challenges of crowdsourced testing are typically centered on logistics and management, while some are people morale and buy-in related. On a quality implementation front, one of the biggest concerns is how to tie in the test effort from a crowdsourced team into the core team's overall test effort and map it to the test strategy to determine whether the exit criteria have been met adequately. With growing global teams these challenges are often imminent, even with core test teams, which now gets further amplified when you have disparate crowd testers across the globe working independently of each other, especially when there is no formal and legal binding between the crowd team and the organization. This thus becomes a big challenge for the test manager or director who is driving the test strategy in preparation for product sign-off. Looking at it from another angle, internalizing the input from the crowd and mapping it to the larger test strategy and what should be the working priorities of the product team based on issues reported by the crowd are practical challenges to face. Seth Eliot, in his presentation on testing in production (leveraging end users for testing) at Software Test Conference 2011,[16] presents varied examples of crowd-sourced testing. He talks about how Swayable.com, a crowd voting plat-form, leverages end users to provide feedback on its site (Figure 4.1). The page asking for end-to-end user feedback is shown in Figure 4.2.

While it is exciting to see the site get end-to-end user feedback through crowdsourced testing, the challenges it faces and needs to address are sifting through the voluminous feedback it receives from users and translating it into actionable work items for the team. Especially when open-ended statements such as "What do you like on this home page?" and "What would you change on this home page?" are asked, the receiver cannot fully rely on automated intelligence to process the results. Specific individuals along with a combination of tools to analyze patterns in user responses will be needed to handle the huge set of feedback, within the limited time on hand.

The other main challenge is around building the right crowd test team. Although we discuss in our definitions that crowdsourced testing is all about bringing in the community at large to test your product,

Figure 4.1 Swayable.com—a crowd voting platform.

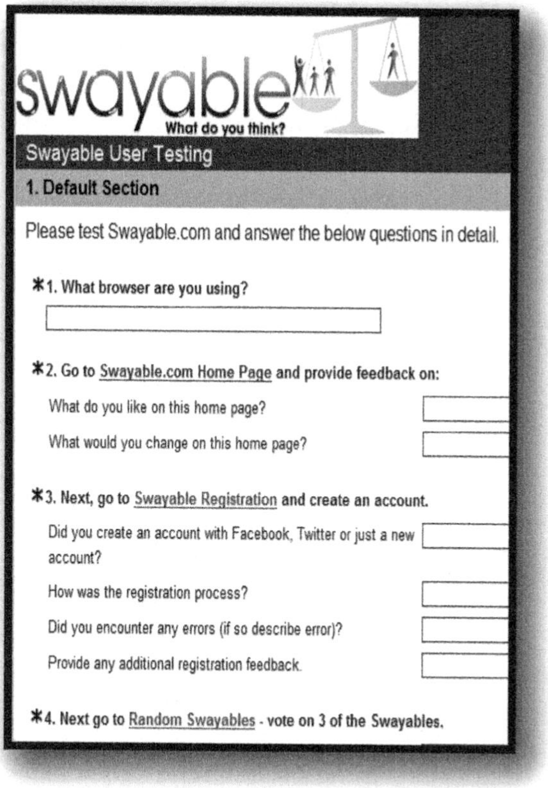

Figure 4.2 How Swayable.com leverages crowd testing.

this is much easier said than done. Identifying the crowdsourced test team can be quite a challenge because although you want diversity, you also want the right crowd testing your product, failing which the overhead of managing the crowd goes up with no significant returns from the test effort. The other side of the issue here is sustaining the identified crowd. This is particularly challenging since the crowd members are not legally bound to work for the organization and can exit the project anytime they are not interested or motivated. So, sustaining the crowd's interest and motivation is a huge challenge for the test team. Another challenge here is building a trusted crowd. Although most often you may not directly know your crowd team, in specific cases, especially when you have concerns around product security and IP, it is better to leverage a trusted crowd that you have worked with in the past and who understand your space really well to get the feedback you value.

Let's take some examples here, again from Seth Eliot's presentation. He talks about how A/B testing, for instance, is a very feasible leveraging crowd tester, as seen in Figure 4.3.

This kind of testing is very powerful, especially when decisions need to be made about design choices, feature inclusions, etc. This is similar to crowd voting in some sense, where the crowd need not think through too much about the solution, but can just base its response on its initial gut. However, this is where it gets challenging for the organization that is crowdsourcing. How does it go about choosing the right crowd here?

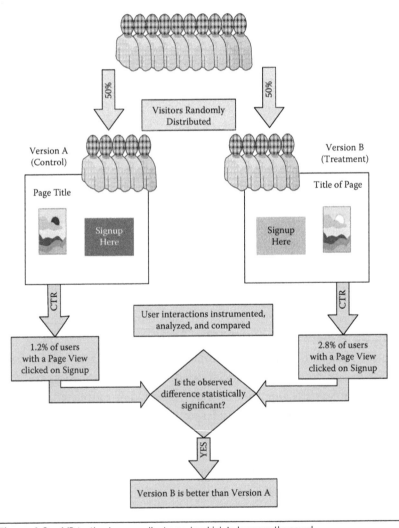

Figure 4.3 A/B testing is an excellent area in which to leverage the crowd.

If I have a wrong crowd that is not relevant for me, evaluating my design and giving me wrong feedback, based on which I decide my action plans, am I not being misguided by the crowd's input? In such open-ended crowd tests, timing is another challenge. How do I know for how long I should keep my A/B tests open to the crowd? Recently, there was an example from Google, where the A/B test results were drastically different when they extended the testing duration and had it run for more time. Had Google made a feature decision based on the results of the first round of A/B tests, the impact would have been quite adverse for Google's business.[17]

Seth also talks in his presentation about a live case where Amazon took end user input in deciding whether to go with a feature that currently is widely used in the online shopping domain. This is the case where an Amazon employee wanted to introduce a recommendations (collaborative filtering engine) feature to offer suggestions to the end user, on additional items to buy, based on what the end user is looking for and what similar other users had bought. In his opinion, this would help sell more items; however, there was resistance for it at an executive level because it might distract end users and affect their conversion rates. Amazon ran a test leveraging the crowd to decide which route to take. The results were overwhelmingly powerful and guided it to the path of incorporating a collaborative filtering engine. Here, again, one of the challenges Amazon might have faced is identifying the right crowd for this experiment—people who are Internet savvy, online shoppers, and in this case, specifically new parents. If we take Google's previous example, Amazon too would have herein faced the challenge on how long the test should have been run to get representative end user results (Figure 4.4).

Figure 4.4   Amazon.com—an early adopter of crowdsourced testing.

The next thing to look at is communication. Communication and associated overhead can become a mounting challenge in a crowd-sourced test effort from two angles:

1. Keeping the entire crowd test team updated on important changes in the product. In the current-day agile world, when things are so dynamic and fast paced, keeping everyone in sync on the changes is difficult even internally. If so, have you thought through the scale of communication challenges you may face when you have to keep the crowd team as well updated? While infrastructure and technology have eased the process of communication significantly, the onus is still on people to decide what, when, and how to communicate, and when you deal with a large team such as a crowd test team, communication can soon become a nightmare.

2. On the same note, since communication needs to be two-way, the challenge is around you not only updating the crowd with important aspects of the product that it needs to know, but also ensuring the crowd is responsive in communicating back to you. Its responses around test results, defects, regressions, and any other questions you may have on its status or test efforts need to be timely and precise yet comprehensive. Getting everyone to provide timely and detailed updates can soon be an unmanageable challenge.

From a security angle, a crowdsourced test effort may face tough challenges on the ground. Safeguarding one's IP, trying to determine who forms your crowd, and whether they have any links with your competitors, are hard challenges that you will have to encounter, gauge the risks and benefits specific to your project, and analyze mitigation strategies for, before you proceed with a full-fledged crowd test effort.

Effective crowdsourcing needs the right amount of time and resources. Despite the fact that the crowd often works independently, as an organization that is spearheading the crowdsourced test effort, you will need to set aside the required amount of time and resources (people who manage the effort, required hardware and software setup typically over the cloud) to engage with the crowd. In the current-day agile world, where time and resources are of essence, organizations may practically find it challenging to support a crowdsourced test effort and may have to devote these resources to other internal test tasks that are of higher priority, although they understand the value the crowd can deliver.

Finally, working with your stakeholders and convincing them that crowdsourced testing is going to reap benefits and add value that outweighs all the challenges discussed above is probably the toughest of them all. Stakeholders are typically concerned around all points mentioned above and, in addition, are also looking at the internal team's morale. Unless the test effort is driven by a series of educated decisions, the internal test team (inclusive of the outsourced test team) may feel threatened when the crowd comes into the picture. Losing out on their confidence and support for project execution is one of the biggest fears for stakeholders, as the internal team forms the backbone of the project at the end of the day. All of these are very valid challenges that you would rather face up front, and work on building a mitigation plan instead of haphazardly encountering them over the course of the project. So, at this stage, understand these from just what the challenges could potentially be. We will discuss solutions that map to each of these challenges in detail in Chapter 5.

Flipping coins, if we look at this from the crowd's angle, while it may face some of the challenges, especially around communication and wholehearted support from the core test team to empower it to succeed, one major challenge it may face is motivation at its own level. What is beginning to happen lately is that amateur crowd testers are beginning to flood the market. They may come in with an intention of making some quick money with quick and dirty testing, so they can target some low-hanging defects in the product. This may totally de-motivate a seasoned tester who is genuinely working toward finding deeper product issues and who is not necessarily reporting as many defects as some of these newer testers. So, it can soon become a battle of quality versus quantity, which is not good for the entire test effort that is under way. On the same note, another challenge that the crowdsourcing company often faces is pricing for crowd testers. If the reward involved is money, what payment strategy should it adopt? Should it pay on a time and material basis, or should it pay them on a service level agreement (SLA) basis driven by specific metrics such as number, priority, and severity of bugs found? Most often the latter case is adopted, but deciding on this depends on the kind of project, what areas are being handed off to the crowd for testing, whether the crowd is a private beta test crowd or an open public crowd, etc. This may be a challenging decision for the organization as it starts this effort, but this is an area where it will soon get a good handle, as it crowdsources a few test projects and gains hands-on experience on what model best suits it.

In this chapter, we have mainly focused on preparing you to be mindful of specific areas of crowdsourced testing that you need to watch out for—be they areas and times when it would not work or challenges/problems that you need to face. Preparing you with these points up front will help you develop an unbiased and objective view into crowdsourced testing and better handle the implementation plan with thought-through strategies to mitigate these challenges. This will be the focus of our discussion in Chapter 5.

Did You Know?

While we looked in detail at the challenges and limitations of crowdsourced testing in this chapter, we would like to leave you pondering over one core point: the difference between *acting* and *using*. Although a crowd user can be brought in for his testing, end user, or subject matter expertise skills, we have already seen that the value in engaging with him is maximized only when he is an end user or a subject matter expert. Arguably, his end user representation is what brings in the most value. While the other representations of a crowd user are also useful, the most important thing to keep in mind is the differentiation between a user and an actor. As a user, you are letting him use the product and provide feedback; whereas as an actor, you are still providing him a script in some shape or form to act like a user. Being cognizant of this difference will go a long way in mitigating the model's limitations and surfacing its core value in a test project.

5

HOW TO SUCCESSFULLY IMPLEMENT CROWDSOURCED TESTING

"Putting Our Differences to Work" by Debbe Kennedy

When asked to come up with their thoughts on leadership best practices, tips, and insights at a Leadership by Example session in 2010, participants shared several messages.[18]

This one by Debbe particularly caught our attention specific to our context on crowdsourced testing. Let us put our differences to work in the context of bringing diversity into the workplace in enhancing the feedback from end users for the product under test. While we have already seen that the crowd succeeds and, in turn, the product benefits when we bring diversity into the mix, just diversity alone is not sufficient in getting you the desired results. We mentioned in Chapter 4 that, despite the benefits crowdsourced testing bears, it has its own set of challenges and limitations that need to be addressed so as to reap the best that the model has to offer. Along with the diversity in the crowd team, the internal team that is driving this effort has to focus on creating and implementing a robust plan (a plan driven by best practices) in building a successful crowdsourced testing effort. In the same leadership session, an anonymous entry read: "A vision without a plan is a hallucination."

This, again, is a very apt saying specific to our needs, because oftentimes the belief is that crowdsourced testing can be put together as a last-minute task with not much advanced planning and you can still benefit from the effort. The truth is that this results in more chaos than value, and if at all you are able to derive value from such a haphazardly put together effort, it is more so due to chance and not mastery or skill that can be replicated.

Figure 5.1 Crowdsourced testing—let's march into a successful implementation.

While the crowd that is working on a testing assignment can choose its own technique to test the product, decide how much time to spend on the testing effort, and make some of these parameters' choices on its own, the overall plan for crowdsourced testing is a very educated decision that the organization makes. It has to understand the *what, when, and how* to crowdsource in a testing effort. These are very important decisions that need to be carefully made, and over time, best practices around these need to be built to align to your needs. Also, these best practices need to be a customized list that you revisit for every such test undertaking because the same set may not be applicable across organizations, across groups, or even between different projects in the same group. If the team that is driving the crowdsourced test effort keeps this in mind as a high-level set of guidelines and is open to incorporating newer practices to meet the needs of every crowdsourced test effort, it will be well on it path to success (Figure 5.1).

Best Practices in Implementing a Successful Crowdsourced Test Effort

We will focus on three main questions in this section:

What do we crowdsource in our testing effort?
When do we crowdsource our testing effort?
How do we crowdsource our testing effort?

Understanding these three areas will give us a very good and comprehensive idea on implementing a crowdsourced test effort. Also, if we were to prioritize this set of three questions, it is important to first understand the when element. Once we do this, the what and how will automatically follow.

When Do We Crowdsource Our Testing Effort?

If you look at this question closely and recall the definitions and examples of crowdsourced testing that we have looked at so far, you will be able to see that a product may not be ready for the crowd's viewing at all times. You need to make a careful choice about when to bring in the crowd from the standpoints of effectiveness of effort and results, product readiness, and team and crowd's morale. Here are some key points to keep in mind in this space. Crowdsource your testing when:

1. **Your product is reasonably ready and functioning end to end:** Crowdsourced testing benefits a lot from getting real end user feedback on features that they use the most. Since typically the end user-facing features and associated integrations fall in place together when the product is almost ready for end-to-end testing, it makes sense to bring in the crowd at this stage. This is a stage where the product is intuitive enough to be played around with and tested on, rather than having the crowd read through product documents to understand the system. In fact, you want your crowd to have a complete end user perspective, and you want to empower them to understand the system as they use it. This is the main reason to bring them in later in the game. For example, we at QA InfoTech leverage the crowd as and when needed for various scenarios, and one very popular case is bringing in the visually challenged users when the product is reasonably ready end to end for getting their realistic accessibility user feedback. While we have a team of accessibility testers working on our assignments, such a crowd that is made up of the visually challenged (for which we work with organizations like the Blind Relief Association in India) paired with our trained accessibility test experts gives us feedback that is very valuable and practical, covering all aspects of accessibility (Figure 5.2).

Figure 5.2 Visually challenged user with an accessibility tester at QA InfoTech.

2. **Your internal team has the time and resources to work on the crowd team's feedback:** Feedback that comes in from the crowd test team needs to be internalized in the product team and acted upon as soon as possible, similar to internal defects that are logged. Oftentimes the internal team is busy with its other product development priorities. This leads to delays in following up on the feedback that the crowd has provided. It is very important to avoid this scenario, for two reasons: first, valuable feedback from the crowd, which is often real end user issues, is being unattended due to such delays; second, and more importantly, if the crowd gets a vibe that its feedback is not being acted on, it may be de-motivated to test your product. This is especially true in cases where the crowd may be testing your product because of its brand loyalty and a sense of inclusion that it is getting to see your product before its release, etc., and is not being paid any monetary compensation. In such cases, the crowd is even more sensitive to factors such as these where its feedback is not being looked into, and it may lose interest in the test effort and soon disintegrate. This is very detrimental to your crowd testing effort, as you have taken painstaking steps to put together a crowd team—a crowd that is diverse, trustworthy, and valuable. So, make it a priority to bring in the crowd only when you know that the crowd's feedback can be internally acted upon within a reasonable time.

3. **You do not have time or resources for a formal in- or outsourced test effort:** Your organization may be a start-up that does not have resources to put together a formal test effort. You may be a large organization, but your release cycle at a certain time may be so very short that you have not had the time to put together a formal test effort. In cases such as these, crowdsourced testing comes in very handy. Although this is not the ideal solution and crowdsourced testing cannot replace a formal test effort (at least at this time), it is a good backup option to get some amount of test coverage, rather than having a product released without any quality coverage at all. For example, in the case below, Microsoft was launching an application named Popfly a few years back (this application is no longer existent in the marketplace). As big a company as Microsoft is, it launched it on a beta testing mode largely leveraging the crowd to test the application given the short release cycle. Regardless of the reasons why such immediate and spike crowdsourced testing may be taken on, organizations need to understand that this is only a temporary solution. A formal test effort by an internal team (whether insourced or outsourced, but one that has a binding responsibility on the product's quality) that takes responsibility for the product's quality cannot be eliminated for the sake of engaging with a crowd test team (Figure 5.3).

4. **Your content files are ready:** If you are planning to leverage the crowd mainly for its subject matter expertise in a certain area on the basis of which your content is developed, then the right time for you to bring in the crowd is when the content files are ready. This is also the case when your crowd is brought in to verify content in a certain locale (where it takes on translation or linguistic verification). Here, again, the timing of engaging with the crowd is important, and it does not help to bring the crowd onto the team in advance.

5. **Ongoing feedback from an SME team is valuable:** If you have a group of subject matter experts (SMEs) in the crowd who you typically engage with from the very beginning so that they provide you feedback on not just your implemented product but also your design, architecture, feature set, etc., it makes

Figure 5.3 Leveraging the crowd when time is of essence.[38]

perfect sense to engage with them throughout the life cycle. But keep in mind that in such cases, the crowd is a very select handpicked crowd with whom you may sign a nondisclosure agreement (NDA) to ensure your product's intellectual property (IP) is secure. Taking the example of Microsoft again, it has a very active SME community that often represents end users in providing ongoing feedback to its products, such as Visual Studio, Share Point, etc. This is a community of crowd testers that actively engages in various stages of the development cycle, often bound by an NDA, getting to see the product from inception to final implementation. From the crowd standpoint, as regular users of these products, an early peek into these newer builds gives them an edge in the marketplace in leveraging the software for their needs (Figure 5.4).

What Do We Crowdsource in Our Testing Effort?

In Chapter 4, we talked about what not to crowdsource in a testing effort. While that would have laid some initial ground for your understanding in this area, let's specifically now look at what to crowdsource in your testing effort, which will help you understand areas that benefit the most from crowdsourced testing.

Figure 5.4   Leveraging the crowd for ongoing SME feedback.[39]

1. **Pick areas where end user feedback would be very valuable** (specifically, end user facing features and associated areas): For example, front-end features and associated user experience are a great space where the crowd can provide valuable feedback. If your product is in a very competitive space, and you have a loyal user base, leverage them to ask for feedback on what they would like to see in a new version's design and feature set. Nothing can match the feedback you directly get from the field.

2. **Pick areas where the crowd's subject matter expertise or local presence is very valuable:** Areas such as content testing (where, say, for example, you bring in a doctor to provide feedback on the usability of a medical application), compatibility testing (where the crowd participates in testing your product for live compatibility across devices, platforms, versions, Internet bandwidths, etc.), localization testing (including linguistic verification), and performance testing (where the crowd takes on device level performance testing in real end user environments) are where the crowd can add a lot of value. If you are able to source together the right crowd to get feedback on these areas, your product will greatly benefit with this live feedback that supplements the internal test team's efforts (Figures 5.5 and 5.6).

Figure 5.5   Leveraging the crowd (e.g., professors) for content grading.[40]

Figure 5.6   Leveraging the crowd for linguistic verification across locales.[41]

3. **Pick areas where you can align any gaps in your testing strategy:** One of the challenges we talked about in Chapter 4 was around the crowd's efforts not aligning with the test strategy, making it a very random choice of tasks to execute. To mitigate this challenge, it is important for the test management team to periodically understand what the internal test coverage is (both from insourced and outsourced test teams) and map it with the larger test strategy to understand what

the gaps are. The gaps should not be assigned to the crowd as is. A further analysis needs to be done to see if these are tasks where the crowd will succeed and accordingly assign it to them. Also, on an ongoing basis, load balancing and task shuffling need to be taken up to determine whether teams are assigned tasks where they will succeed, and accordingly make, any changes as needed. This will create a win-win scenario for everyone since the results will now be in line with the test strategy and you will also have a motivated team that works on tasks that empower it to succeed.

How Do We Crowdsource Our Testing Effort?

Having looked at the questions of when and what to crowdsource in a test effort, let's move on to look at the third question: How do we crowdsource our testing effort? By now you may have spent time thinking about the what and when of crowdsourcing specific to your test needs. In this section, there are several point to consider:

1. **Think about how to put together a crowd team:** We earlier talked about one of the challenges being hiring and sustaining the right crowd team. This can be as simple as bringing in a small and relevant extended team from outside your core team but still within your organization to test your product, while on the other end of the spectrum, it could be as complex as bringing in global crowd testers whom you have never seen, met, or interacted with before. You need to think about how to reach out to the global crowd to be able to pick your relevant testers. Are you going to run a promotion on your website? This may get you some attention, but not as much as you need. Think creatively on how to market your needs to draw the attention of your relevant crowd. Think of running a promotion campaign on your LinkedIn or Facebook page; promote your message on the need for crowd testers on Twitter or any other social platform that you have a presence on with active followers. These are excellent places where you have built your brand loyalty that you should now leverage. Tap in to your past crowd testing team if you have had one such program. If you are a large organization, run an internal campaign to find crowd testers.

Once you have drawn their attention, keep the registration process simple. You want to engage with the crowd as soon as you can and do not want to be wasting time and losing out on the members' interest by asking them a number of questions about themselves. However, in some specific scenarios where you are running a private beta or your IP needs confidentiality, you may want to interact with your crowd testers and also gauge their appropriateness to work on your product by a short interview, say, on Skype or a video platform, for you to confirm their genuineness—this is what we call the trusted crowd. This is a crowd that you have directly vetted and handpicked like your internal team, although it may not have been as rigorous as that. Building such a trusted team is becoming more and more important by the day, especially in cases where there is payment involved for the testing they do for you. Building the right crowd team is not an easy task; it requires regular monitoring, even at times when the crowd is not working on your project, to ensure your database of crowd testers is not obsolete.

2. **Identify the right person to drive the crowd testing effort:** Crowd testing is not a process that involves throwing tasks over the fence to a team of testers who will work on your needs and return results. Although you want to let the crowd operate creatively and independently in it space, it is important to have a dedicated person or a team (if it is a larger effort) drive your crowd testing effort. This person is typically a program/project manager or a tester who is passionate about engaging the crowd to improve the product's richness and quality. This is a person who is excited about working with the crowd, who can draw meaningful inferences from crowd actions that may sometimes be randomizing, who can serve as a good liaison between the internal team and the crowd and be result oriented with both groups of people, who can motivate the crowd and keep its excitement level about the product high, who is savvy enough on what, when, and how much to communicate with the crowd, and who has very good and effective communication skills.

3. **Empower the person driving the crowd test effort to succeed:** Having identified the right person or team to take charge of the crowd testing effort, it is important to now

empower this person to succeed. Keep in mind that if he/the team succeeds, your crowd as well as your overall crowd test effort succeeds. So aspects such as the right tools for communication (use of knowledge management systems, wiki kind of portals, etc.), the cloud to enable ease of sharing builds, virtual private clouds as needed to promote security and control access, etc., all need to be looked at in this stage. While the person identified should be able to drive and make choices on most of these fronts, from your side, see if any management help is needed to expedite permissions, as some of these may be needed at very short notice to reach out to the crowd.

4. **Decide if your crowd needs to communicate with one another:** We had earlier discussed that the crowd is most successful when it operates independently. However, there could be scenarios when it makes sense to facilitate communication among the crowd players. For example, imagine you are conducting a private beta with a very select group of crowd users/testers and your product is still under development where you want to give them ongoing updates on newer features, functionality, and answer queries they may have, especially when your product is architecturally complex in nature. In such cases, it makes sense to have the crowd participate in a group conference call using, say, a web video platform where they get direct updates from you and are also able to get a view into questions that others have, which will expedite their understanding of your system. This is especially the case when the crowd is an SME team that works with you throughout your development life cycle, engaged from even the early days of design. On the other hand, if you consider a case where you are building a very intuitive and easy-to-understand web application (say, a social networking application) for which you have built a global crowd team, it does not make any sense to get the crowd to communicate with one another. This will only increase your overhead, will not give you any value, and in fact, will bring down the resultant value as the crowd will trespass into each other's creativity if they are allowed to cross-communicate. Deciding on whether the crowd should communicate with each other or not is thus a very selective choice that needs to be taken up on a case-by-case basis.

5. **Win your stakeholder's approval:** Like in any project, winning the stakeholder's approval is a key for a crowdsourced test effort. This is such an important space that we have dedicated a separate chapter for this topic (Chapter 7), along with winning the rest of the team's support. At this stage keep in mind that the stakeholders often have several concerns in bringing in a crowdsourced test team due to their lack of understanding on what crowdsourcing is all about or due to some very genuine concerns (most of which we discussed under the section on challenges in crowdsourced testing in Chapter 4). We will discuss this topic in detail along with winning your overall team's support into the crowd testing effort in Chapter 7.

6. **Identify your crowd's motivators:** We have already discussed that money is not the only variable that motivates the crowd. There could be several other variables, such as transparency into your products before market release, brand loyalty, community fun, etc. Determining the motivators and categorizing them in buckets will help you determine groups of crowd testers, what tasks to engage them on, and how to sustain their interest levels and better engage them in the long run. In fact, there are quite a bit of psychological and software angles in crowd user management where you can leverage management theories such as Maslow's hierarchy of needs to build a good motivation matrix. At a high level, if you look at the matrix in Figure 5.7, the self-actualization, self-esteem, and safety buckets are typically excellent motivators for the crowd when you take on crowdsourced testing because these are driven by one's quest for professional excellence, money, and a sense of satisfaction getting to see the product before the market does. For example, the ones we have underlined in Figure 5.7 are typically drivers that motivate the crowd.

7. **Pick tasks that motivate your crowd:** Having identified your crowd and what motivates it, you also need to look into what tasks to assign the crowed such that its members would be motivated to work on them. We have already looked at what to crowd test, but it would be a wise call to randomly pick those tasks and assign them to the crowd. For example, let's say

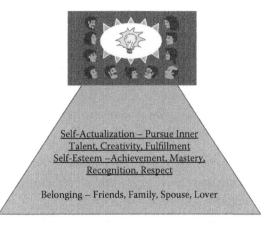

Figure 5.7   Maslow's hierarchy of needs in determining crowd's motivators.[42]

your testing needs span localization and mobile performance testing areas and you have linguistic experts from remote parts of Africa that have signed up for crowd testing. However, they do not have access to mobile devices of your needs. It only makes sense for you to assign the localization testing to them, whereas you need to look at some other group of testers/users for the mobile performance testing. Mapping tasks to the crowd's capabilities and motivators will go a long way in setting you up for success. We will discuss this in greater detail when we move on to the next section to talk about examples and a work model that will set you up for success.

Examples: Practical Implementations of Crowdsourced Testing

Nothing explains a concept better than examples. While we have seen some examples along the way on crowdsourced testing and its implementation, we'll devote this section to examples. We'll look at varied forms in which crowdsourced testing has been used, varied organizations (services, products) that have used it, and why and how they were successful in specific cases, which will give you a very good picture of the model's implementation at work.

At QA InfoTech, we are a test outsourcing services provider. However, we have augmented our services portfolio to include crowdsourced testing in varied forms to benefit both our clients and us, and below are some scenarios where we have been using this model.

We have recently built a crowdsourced testing platform to help us take the benefits of the crowd to our clients who may have a need to test varied mobile devices, locales, and performance bandwidths covering test areas such as functionality, UI, usability, accessibility, globalization, and performance. This is a platform that empowers a crowd tester working remotely to execute his tasks in an organized manner. Some of the core features this platform provides include:

1. Enable a tester to register himself on our crowd test platform
2. View past, current, and upcoming events (crowd test activities) and register for events of his choice
3. Start the testing process for a registered event when the event opens
4. View bugs logged by others (to minimize chances of duplicate bugs), log a new bug, and view his overall bug statistics
5. View the overall money earned on individual and group crowd test events
6. View the star testers who are doing very well on varied crowd test events
7. Administrative features around managing the overall platform

The platform's features have been designed keeping in mind that the crowd would be a remote team and that there would be challenges around communication, getting responses from the members, and motivating the crowd on an ongoing basis to continue testing on our platform, especially if they have now become a trusted crowd that we can rely on.

When we built this platform, we obviously had a team of testers validate and verify the implementation in case of any product development life cycle. However, we also went a step ahead to bring in our internal crowd (QA InfoTech's employees) to test this platform. We made it a 2.5-hour event over a weekend, had our internal crowd register for the event by paying a small subscription fee, and used that money to finally distribute the prize money to the winners. The results from this exercise were phenomenal. We had testers from varied levels in the organization take a stab at the platform, with their major motivators being earning some small additional income (if they win the contest), having fun with their coworkers, gaining visibility across the entire company, and above all, a willingness to help the company.

Figures 5.8 to 5.11 are some snapshots from the platform (the platform is internal to the organization at this time and will be launched to the crowd community soon).

The results from the exercise were very encouraging, where we had over 200 testers join in, and within 2.5 hours, they reported

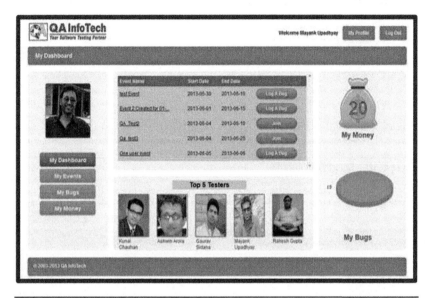

Figure 5.8 Portal's home page listing the various crowd testing events.

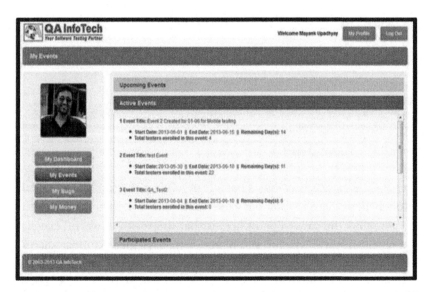

Figure 5.9 Event listing in detail.

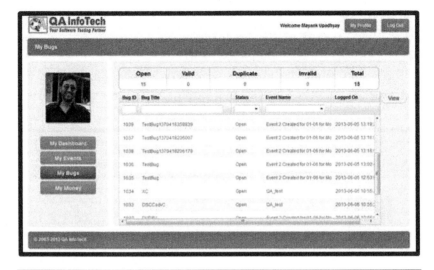

Figure 5.10 Defects dashboard.

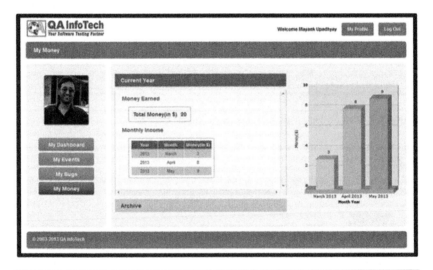

Figure 5.11 Money dashboard.

over 3000 issues. It was thus a herculean task for the triage team to sift through all of them to filter out valid issues and rank them to determine the winners. The case in point here is that this was a powerful exercise demonstrating the wisdom of crowds, which yielded us great success even when done internally in the organization. All it called for was the right planning, setting the right expectations with the crowd, stakeholder buy-in, and a team to drive the effort end to end. This was a great success of an external crowdsourced testing platform that was tested by an internal crowd.

Similarly, a few other cases where we have using crowdsourced testing at our company include:

1. Leveraging the visually challenged people from the Blind Relief Association in India. We have trained these people from a software testing angle to take on accessibility testing. These people are now a representative set of end users and testers who, along with our accessibility test experts, are able to generate a lot of value for our clients (discussed further earlier in this chapter).

2. Pooling in our internal testers/employees for mobile testing on a varied set of devices (smartphones, tablets, e-readers, etc.) through a rental model. Depending on the device and the time the employee gives his device for testing, we determine the rental compensation to be given out. This helps us enhance our test coverage for our clients, without investing in expensive devices where the return on investment is not very high, given that they become obsolete quite soon.

3. Content grading for specific subject matter expertise sourcing experts across domains (such as doctors, professors) through our partnerships with various universities.

These show you specific cases of how we have leveraged crowdsourced testing across its manifestations (internal sourcing, sourcing subject experts and end users through partnerships) and how it was done by a services company of not a very large scale (we are about 700 people strong as of this writing).

Moving on to look at product companies, several companies have been using crowdsourced testing, not necessarily now, but for the last several years, although it was called varied names (beta testing—public, private, etc.). We all know how Gmail was in beta for a really long time. That is nothing but crowd testing, and Google is known to release new ideas quickly to the audience and have them in beta for quite sometime to leverage end user feedback.

We have talked quite a bit about crowd motivators, and that it is important to identify the right motivators and align tasks that match with the crowd's motivational pieces. To make this easier to implement at the workplace, here is a model that has been used by a test director,

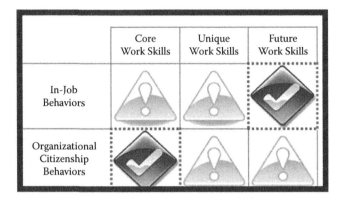

Figure 5.12 Model to help determine successful engagements with the crowd.[43]

Ross Smith, at Microsoft on quite a few internal crowdsourced testing projects. Microsoft is a big believer in crowdsourced testing, via both beta testing (public and private) and using its internal crowd of diverse users. So, understanding how this model is used there will definitely help ease our understanding of the motivational pieces in a crowdsourced test implementation. This model is represented in Figure 5.12.

Going by the Y-axis in the figure, in-job behavior is a behavior that the employee demonstrates as part of his core job responsibilities. Organizational citizenship behavior is something that a person demonstrates as a good Samaritan in the organization—something that is not required as part of his core responsibilities, but he is willing to demonstrate due to his goodwill for and vested interest in the organization.

On the X-axis, let us look at work skills:

1. **Core work skills** are skills that a vast majority of the population would have—for example, the ability to speak a certain language, to know how to use the Internet for regular web browsing.
2. **Unique work skills** are skills that an individual possesses for which he has been tasked with the job at hand—for example, the individual's experience with a certain test automation tool, experience with a certain programming language.
3. **Future work skills** are skills that an individual needs to grow into through formal and informal education, work experience, etc.—for example, learning a new programming language or a tool or a technique.

In Ross's model, he talks about how productivity games yield maximum success when they are built for:

1. In-job behavior working on future work skills
2. Organization citizenship behavior working on core work skills

For the sake of our discussion on crowd, we are more interested in the second scenario of organization citizenship behavior; to be fool-proof, though, let's look at an example for the in-job behavior as well. Let's take an example of a typist who already types at a certain speed per hour. If a game were to be built for the typist to type at that speed + x, the game's results are going to be conflicting with the person's core job responsibilities, and thus confusing to the player on what kind of performance to demonstrate. Since typing is a unique skill for the typist, it does not make sense to build productivity games in this space. Rather, if the typist is challenged with a future work skill where he or she does not just type out content but also drafts content in some scenarios, it is a clear avenue for growth. Building a game in this space will make it both exciting and motivating for the individual with specific outcomes and rewards to expect. Ross's full paper, "The Future of Work Is Play," is available on a site that he runs focusing on management innovation.[44]

Extending this same concept to practical use, Microsoft has successfully leveraged its internal crowd in two scenarios for phenomenal test results:

1. **Language quality game:** During Windows 7 testing, Microsoft leveraged its diverse set of international employees for localization testing across 36 languages. This was in addition to its core linguistic testing efforts, yielding it a huge success of over 4600 players that voluntarily signed up, 530,000+ screens that were reviewed, and 6700+ bugs that were reported. Here the crowd's motivators were getting to see Windows 7 before it was released to the market and a loyalty in contributing to their own company.

2. **Communicate hope:** Players across Microsoft were leveraged for dog fooding (beta testing) Office Communicator, an enterprise messaging tool, with an incentive of contributing to disaster relief agencies through the points they earn. Herein, the motivator that was touched was a soft one on

the crowd's philanthropic and social cause wants, to direct their test efforts into tangible contributions for disaster relief agencies of their choice.

In both these cases, Microsoft leveraged the core skills and the organizational citizenship behavior of its diverse internal crowd to bring in additional test coverage on top of the formal testing efforts.

Several other companies, such as Netflix, Amazon, and Google, use crowdsourced testing regularly, whether in the form of contests or beta testing projects.

Engagement Models in Leveraging a Crowdsourced Test Effort

Using the right engagement model is an important factor for success. In ongoing project execution, the question would be around whether to engage a full-time internal team or to bring in contractors. If the work is being outsourced, the question would be around whether to have the team on-site, nearshore, or offshore. While some of these questions typically do not arise in a crowdsourced test effort, as the team is almost always remotely located, there is a different question to answer here. This question is around the engagement model when it comes to compensating them. We have discussed in quite a few places over the course of the book so far that money is not always the motivator that drives the crowd to contribute to the testing effort. However, in situations where money is involved, what are the engagement models that are used? The most commonly used model is the service level agreement (SLA)-driven pay per use kind of model where the crowd tester is paid based on the deliverables submitted. Herein, the deliverable that is largely used to determine how much the tester will be paid is defects. The number of defects is not a significant consideration when compared to the validity of the defects. $X per valid defect is the most commonly used model so that the company leveraging the crowd has control on the ROI it is reaping, especially when it has not seen these crowd testers and when they work remotely. There are a few other protocols the organization has to clear up front in this space. Unlike the traditional testers who have access to the defect database where they can see who filed what defect and when, these crowd testers usually work in isolation. So, what if a tester were to file a defect that has already been reported by another tester. The defect may be a perfectly valid one, but since it has already been found by someone else, it is a duplicate. Does this affect how the tester is paid, or do you still pay him because it is a unique valid defect from his standpoint. These are important scenarios the organization needs to sort out before engaging with the crowd. We will look at these in greater detail in Chapter 6 on defect management in crowdsourced testing. For now, keep in mind that paying testers for valid bugs they file is one of the most popular engagement models. The other models, which are not so very popular but which are still in use, include:

1. **Pay by the hour** (similar to a time and material contract in a vendor relationship): This can be used when you are using the crowd to give you other artifacts than just defects, such as test cases, plans, etc. Or in situations where you know they are going to add value by the suggestions and feedback they have for your product, especially when they are a known crowd (more like a private beta), this model will work well, so you don't have to track each defect from a payment standpoint and can use those numbers just to gauge their performance.

2. **Pay a predetermined flat amount** (similar to a fixed-bid contract in a vendor relationship): Typically, this is not a very common model in crowdsourced testing, since you do not want to commit a flat price to a crowd that is not working under your direct control. Mapping its value to the efforts it puts in will be a challenge if you were to go this route. However, here again, if you really know the crowd to be a subject matter expert, and, say, for example, you want it to take on linguistic verification, you could explore paying it a fixed price or based on the number of words to verify, as opposed to defects found.

These two models are not so commonly used in crowdsourced testing mainly because the organization does not have objective ways to measure the crowd's performance when the payment is left open ended; this is why the pay per valid bug found is a more popular engagement model. Understand who your crowd is, what tasks you would engage it on, for how long, the ease of sharing your defect database with your crowd, what past relationship you have with it, etc., in determining the right payment engagement model that will work for you.

As we close this chapter, it is worth the reiteration that although a crowdsourced testing effort may be an informal one (in terms of how the crowd tests your product/application), it takes a lot of careful planning in implementing the test effort. These practices also mitigate all the challenges that we have discussed so far, helping an organization reap the maximum ROI from the crowd, and all the examples we have seen in this chapter are added cases that help reinforce that crowdsourced testing is indeed possible even with the tight constraints that most projects operate within.

Did You Know?[D-6]

The right level of engagement is important not just for internal employees, but also for the crowd. Here are three quick takeaways on building an effective engagement strategy with the crowd:

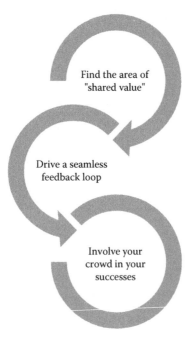

Find the area of "shared value"

Drive a seamless feedback loop

Involve your crowd in your successes

6

Defect Management in Crowdsourced Testing

Just because you've counted all the trees doesn't mean you've seen the forest.

—Anonymous[45]

The quote very effectively sums up the mind-set of why you need crowd testers testing your product and reporting issues. No doubt that you may have a very capable test team (be it internal, outsourced, or a combination of both). However, the additional test coverage that the crowd brings in due to its test expertise, domain know-how, or end user representation is of great value add, as we have seen in the previous chapters. When it comes to implementation practices in engaging with a crowd, we saw a core set of best practices in Chapter 5. However, given the importance of defect management, we decided to dedicate one chapter purely to crowdsourced testing defect management. This is an area that can often make or break a test team's relationship with the rest of the product team and also impact product quality, either positively or negatively, making this a very important area of discussion. We will start off talking about some core problems and challenges in any defect management effort, and then move on to defect management, specifically in the crowdsourced testing space. To promote easier understanding, we will organize this chapter as a series of questions and answers, anticipating the questions you all may have as readers.

What Is Defect Management?

A tester testing a product or an application, reporting defects, and regressing fixed issues is often considered to be doing defect management. But in a tester's role this is only one part of the overall defect

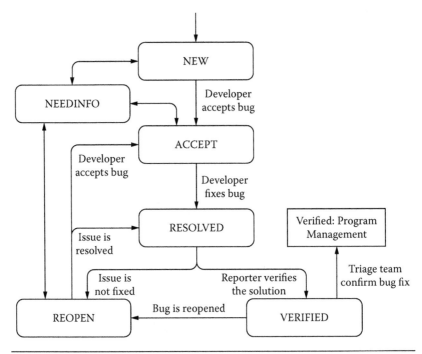

Figure 6.1 Defect management life cycle.[19]

management cycle. This is a very important piece, because the filed defect is what initiates the entire defect management cycle. The defect then flows from filing to triage to fixing (if the bug has been accepted for a fix) to sanity testing at the developer's end to regression at the tester's end, before the defect's life is complete. Another important step could also be to create test cases specific to this defect if it does not map to an existing test case. This due diligence from the tester helps ensure the defect has been addressed fully, including considering it for subsequent milestones and releases, by including the new test as part of the regression suite. Pictorially, this life cycle is shown in Figure 6.1.

What Are Some Core Challenges in Defect Management in a Product Team?

Defect management is an important cord that ties the entire team together. As previously mentioned, it can either make or break not just the quality of the product, but also the team's morale and bonding among themselves. Defect management is thus a product team's task as a whole and not just that of the test team, although the test team has a larger share to play.

From an implementation level, the challenges are often around:

1. **Establishing process understanding:** Defect management calls for the right level of process understanding among the entire product team. In most teams, a process may not have even been defined, which can lead to a lot of chaos, when each team player follows his own processes. Defect management is a life cycle that calls for a very detailed implementation plan that the entire product team needs to understand. This is critical because bugs are filed not just by testers. Oftentimes, there are others, including the developers themselves, who file defects, and it is important for everyone to understand what the processes are to maintain consistency in the defect management life cycle.

2. **Implementing the defined processes consistently:** Just having an implementation plan is not sufficient. In most teams, the challenge is around consistently adhering to the defined processes. The team has to buy in to the usefulness of the processes, which will help successfully roll them out. Oftentimes, teams start off with a bang and very soon start drifting away from the defined limits, especially when multiple disciplines across geographies are expected to use them.

3. **Making the right decisions in a proactive manner as an individual and as a group:** While processes are a defined set of guidelines to help bring consistency and discipline into the implementation plan, team members need to use their individual decision-making capabilities in specific scenarios rather than sticking to guidelines to the T. This is more of a challenge when teams are working remotely and decisions need to be made on the fly. For instance, a triage team (that reviews bugs and decides on the course of action) may be running lean on a given day. The person who is around will have to make the right decision on behalf of the team, taking into account the interests of the entire product team and, more importantly, the quality

of the product under development. Similarly, a tester who is working remotely has to be judicious on what to include in a bug, whether to club a few issues together, and make his own call rather than completely relying on the process guideline.

4. **Maintaining thoroughness in filing defects:** This is an important step in defect management. The entire team has to understand what needs to be included in a defect to make it precise and complete yet not overwhelming to the reader. This is a skill that is developed over time taking into account what the group needs and the group's working style. As a person who is reporting the defect, though, one has to think through to see what the reader as well as the developer (who fixes the bug) will need, to include them proactively. For example, if I am working remotely, would including a video of the defect reproduction make it easier for the team to see the issue rather than just providing a series of written steps/instructions to follow? While finding defects calls for special skills, thoroughness in defect filing and subsequent management goes a long way in differentiating a top-notch tester from the rest.

5. **Sticking to a prompt and timely handshake in handling defects:** It is becoming increasingly important in the best interest of the product and the team to have timelines and service level agreements (SLAs) around timelines in defect management included in the process guidelines. The team has to be disciplined in following them too, as in the absence of such discipline, there could be instances where an action is pending on a certain person that is holding up the entire defect management process. Say, for instance, the developer has fixed the bug while the tester has not taken the time to regress it; the process all of a sudden is halted due to the dependency on a single individual, which again affects both the product quality and the team's morale. While processes can build in some flexibility to accommodate the team's dynamics, a rigid SLA is often important to ensure promptness and a smooth handshake among team members in defect management.

From a team psychology standpoint, the challenges are around:

1. **Bringing in a personal element to defect management and losing objectivity:** The product team often is very attached to every defect that it files. A team that is not seasoned and mature can quickly lose objectivity around defect reporting and can take every bug very personally. A tester might feel offended if a bug he reported is not taken up for a fix. A developer might feel discouraged looking at bugs in his module and may take them personally as a representation of his bad work on the product development side. A requirements bug might offend the business team since it defined the requirements. At all levels, even people with several years of experience might sometimes lose sight of the big picture and take defect management to a totally personal level, which is very detrimental to the product quality and team morale. The triage team herein plays a very important role in ensuring that the right checks and balances are in place on an ongoing basis, and that the team maintains objectivity in the overall defect management process. For instance, if a defect has not been taken up for a fix, the tester needs to understand the constraints within which the triage team made a decision, rather than looking at it as a personal offense to him and the defect he filed.

2. **Considering defect management as an overhead:** Given the steps involved in defect management, especially setting up a triage team and ensuring it meets regularly at varying frequencies, depending on the stage in the product life cycle and the commitment it takes from several team members to get this engine running smoothly, the team may soon lose its motivation and see this exercise as an overhead. This is all the more true when the filed defects lack clarity, are false alarms, the reporters get very defensive about their bugs, etc. The test and product management team herein need to step in to ensure the process is foolproof and, at the same time, not very overwhelming for the participants to maximize on the return on investment (ROI).

Is Defect Management Any Different in a Crowdsourced Test Effort?

While the concept of defect management and the core practices remain the same even in a crowdsourced test effort, there are some differences one needs to keep in mind. The differences mainly stem from the following areas:

1. **A possible remote location of the crowd testers:** Unless an internal crowd in the same location of the core team is leveraged, in most cases even when the company's own employees form the crowd team, they are located remotely from the core project team. Defect management calls for its own discipline and rigor, which makes it more challenging to enforce in a crowd test effort.

2. **Crowd testers are not bound by the internal defect management processes:** There is no legal binding in engaging with the crowd except for a nondisclosure agreement (NDA) that is signed in some cases. Defect management processes that are enforced on an internal team are difficult to enforce with an external crowd because of this reason. That said, the crowd that is participating is a motivated crowd that comes in to test due to its loyalty, commitment, and sometimes money that it gets from you. So, its members may be willing to leverage the existing defect management processes to help you and themselves with a smooth testing cycle.

3. **Crowd testers are not always exposed to defects filed by others:** An internal team has complete access to the defect management system. They are able to see not just their defects, but also defects filed by others, the complete resolution cycle, the history of the issue, past co-relations from other milestones, if any, etc., helping the tester get a 360-degree view into defects, the processes, the level of details he needs, and any other customized information. However, these are details the crowd tester often lacks. In most cases, the crowd may not even be able to see bugs filed by others in the same module that they may be testing. Bear in mind, while you may want to do this to maintain complete confidentiality in the process of working with the crowd, this will lead to a lot of

overhead (for both the crowd and the triage team) in dealing with duplicate and known issues leading to unwanted false alarms. This not only increases the team's overhead, but also brings down everyone's morale, including their confidence on the value of a crowdsourced testing effort. So, even if the full system is not exposed to the crowd, it makes sense to partially expose a relevant section of defects to help the crowd understand the system and its quality better, along with reducing the chances of duplicate and other invalid defects.

4. **Lack of crowd's representation in the triage team:** A triage team that reviews defects and resolves them usually has representation from across teams, including the test team. As a best practice, it is usually recommended to have testers sit in on these triage meetings on a rotational basis so they are exposed to the processes, the discussions, and the expectations of the triage team. This not only helps the tester represent the test team in the triage meeting, but also helps him improve his own performance. Getting a chance to sit on these triage meetings is a great exposure for everyone, including the tester. Since this is a very internal process, the crowd does not get to be part of the triage process, unless it is a very select crowd (like a private beta) where a separate triage could be done for the crowd's bugs. While we want to maintain as much independence as possible in a crowd tester's workflow to bring in as much value as possible, the internal team has to empathize that they often work with very little background on the processes, product, and other defects, and that they should help in possible ways to empower them to succeed. If this means sharing known issues, top issues of the month, high-level expectations of the triage team, a quick view into the triage process, etc., via a limited dashboard view, they should take the time to do so early in the engagement cycle.

5. **Lack of a formal closure on defects filed by the crowd:** While most teams see the value in getting the crowd's feedback, whether through a formal test cycle or through surveys, they are often not diligent enough to close the loop with them on the status of defects. Not doing so puts the crowd at

a disadvantage of not getting a full view into the defects they filed. More importantly, it puts the core product team at a disadvantage of not being disciplined about its defect management process and potentially adversely impacting the crowd's morale and involvement too.

While most of these differences pose additional challenges in defect management in engaging with the crowd, the creativity it brings in, in the defects it files, including the true end user representation, is totally worth the additional overhead. All it calls for is a slightly different thought process to understand how the crowd works and aligning the defect management process to help it succeed rather than using the same internal defect management processes. We will look at some of these implementation practices in the next couple of sections.

What Can Go Wrong If Defect Management Is Not Effective Specific to Crowdsourced Testing?

Defect management is an art and science. It is a science to the extent that it needs specific processes and protocols to maintain a consistent workflow. It is an art to the extent that outside of the core defined processes, it needs the entire team's creativity and smartness in making decisions on the fly, to derive value from the core defect management workflow to benefit the quality of the product. The team as a whole needs to understand this, and when defect management is not effective (whether from a process, process implementation, or team buy-in standpoint), the quality of both the product and the team morale takes a severe hit. From a crowdsourced test effort angle, since an external entity, i.e., the crowd, is involved, if defect management is not a planned and thought-out exercise, it may impact the entire team and the crowd from the following angles:

1. More chaos, especially since the crowd's identity is not very visible to everyone on the team
2. More duplicate issues and false alarms
3. Increased overhead and iterations, including communication challenges
4. Decreased motivation levels for everyone

5. Slips in product timelines and cost elements
6. A de-motivated crowd that might disintegrate from the testing effort
7. Complex triage meetings with random discussions

Can I Leverage Best Practices in Defect Management from a Formal Testing Effort in My Crowdsourced Testing?

To a large extent, best practices from an internal defect management effort can be extended to a crowdsourced test effort too. The point to keep in mind is that some customization is needed when compared to an internal defect management workflow, and the process cannot be leveraged completely as is. As a byline, the mantra should be keep it simple. The crowd is often helping out in your test effort because of its commitment and brand loyalty, or for fun, or for some small monetary gains. Also, given that its members do not have complete visibility into your product, do not complicate the process for them. See if you can give them a simple dashboard to make their defect management workflow more manageable and customized, where they can see the bugs they have filed, their statuses, and also a list of known issues and existing defects that they can look into before reporting their bugs.

Communicate on an ongoing basis: Communication is the key. The person driving the crowd effort should be in touch with the crowd members, either 1:1 or on group conference calls, especially if they do not have access to the common defect database due to confidentiality reasons. Also, since the crowd is not part of the defect triage process, ongoing communication is very important to help its members understand specific scenarios where their bugs were not accepted for a fix.

Brief them on the defect management process and triage expectations: This is important so that you are not enforcing it on them. This, again, may be an additional overhead, but will go a long way in setting the right expectations and help them understand your internal challenges. Create a shorter version (a 1- or 2-page) guideline to help them file defects consistently and establish core protocols around defect filing and regression.

Be prompt in following up on the crowd's bugs: As discussed previously, sometimes the team is busy in its core day-to-day activities, and since it does not directly meet the crowd, it may not work on its defects on priority. However, we have already seen how this might affect the crowd's motivation and also impact product quality adversely. So, as a best practice, the internal team should set aside time to work on the crowd's defects on a prompt basis, realizing that it is a mutual handshake in successfully wading through the defects in enhancing product quality, especially when working with the crowd.

Are Defect Tracking and Measurement Important in Crowdsourced Testing Too?

"You can't manage what you don't measure."[46] This quote very effectively conveys the message of this section. Defect tracking, along specific metrics and measuring the team's performance based on those metrics, is critical to understanding product quality, how the team is performing (not just the test team, but across disciplines), and look for improvement areas overall. It also gives indicators on which modules need more testing focus, where additional resources need to be dedicated, who are some of the best performers on the team, etc. The test management team makes its sign-off call based on measures and associated metrics, of which defect management is a core piece. Given that defect tracking and measurement are so critical in a formal test effort, their importance automatically permeates into a crowdsourced test effort too. While we understand that a crowd test effort is not as formal as an internal focused test effort, we know that the crowd can be an internal crowd, domain experts, testers, or end users. So, while not all of the same metrics will be useful, metrics around the following areas are definitely valuable in understanding the value from the crowd test effort, who are the crowd users who are faring better than the others, and determining what kind of payments need to be given to varied crowd users based on performance, what areas to leverage crowd testing for, whether the implementation plan is effective or not, etc. Again, the goal is to subtly and selectively introduce whatever internal practices are being followed to the crowd such that the value is reaped without randomizing any of the entities involved. The following metrics are definitely very useful in a crowd test effort and are worth sharing selectively with the crowd to help them understand how they are faring:

1. Bugs per tester versus valid bugs per tester (herein, if the crowd is not exposed to the existing defect database, you should not account for duplicate bugs as invalid bugs)
2. Number of valid bugs per tester by priority and severity
3. A rating around the level of detail and articulation provided by the tester since he or she works remotely
4. Measures around the real end user value brought to the table (which is one of the biggest reasons to crowd test your work)
5. Measures around time taken to manage a defect (from filing all the way to closure) to understand both the tester and the internal team's promptness

As a person who drives the crowd test effort, one should keep in mind that while tracking defects and measuring them are important in crowdsourced testing too, the goals are very different here. You are not striving to improve the performance of the tester. Your goal is primarily to focus on enhancing product quality, look for process improvements, if any, use the results to see if the internal team can do better in any way, and understand who among the crowd is faring better than the others so you can motivate, recognize, and remunerate them (if money is involved in your crowd testing effort) better. As a side benefit, when you do these, the crowd tester's individual performance is also often enhanced.

Are There Any Case Studies to Help Understand Crowdsourced Testing Defect Management in Real Time?

In the example we discussed in Chapter 5, where we took on an internal crowdsourced testing effort of our crowd platform, at QA InfoTech, the testing cycle lasted for only 2.5 hours, but the defect management process we undertook therein definitely has good practices that one can leverage and take back to his or her own work environment. As a quick recap, we hosted a crowdsourced test contest inviting our employees to register for participating in the testing effort of a crowdsourcing platform we built. The registration money was used to distribute the prize money among our employees. We had over 200 employees sign up and report over 3000 issues in about 2.5 hours time. Some best practices before, during, and after this crowd test event, which will be useful to look at, include:

1. Create a simple document sharing defect logging guidelines, access mechanisms, and rules for the crowd testing event.
2. Communicate regularly with the testers during the event, to keep them informed of progress, but not randomizing them or overwhelming them with details.
3. Assemble a small team that is available to answer any questions from the crowd, on the spot.
4. Follow the same guidelines regardless of whether the tester is an entry-level employee or a CxO in the organization.
5. Ensure prompt communication soon after the event, on the event details, how many bugs were logged, and how many participated, along with updates on when to expect results.
6. Hold immediate triage meetings to sift through the 3000+ bugs while the issues are still fresh in the eyes of the internal evaluation team.
7. Define clear criteria up front on how bugs will be ranked.
8. Maintain transparency with the crowd on defect statistics and evaluation criteria.
9. Announce results within 3–4 days of the event to show that the internal team values the crowd's bugs as well as is determined to address them seriously in improving product quality.

Since this was a crowdsourced test contest, the team was very aggressive and transparent in the above-mentioned activities. If this is the level of activity that is required for a 2.5-hour crowd test effort, one can only imagine what it would take in an ongoing crowd test effort. Understanding that crowdsourced test effort calls for diligent planning and implementation in all areas, including defect management, and that customization is required rather than sticking to the core internal practices will go a long way in ensuring a smooth defect life cycle that enhances product quality as well as holding the team's (including the crowd) motivation high.

Did You Know?[D-7]

Determining the right crowd size is important from the standpoints of both the diversity of defects you are looking for and defect management. Adding more crowd testers will most definitely yield a greater number of bugs, but will most often also increase the number of duplicate and invalid defects, unless you have a clear defect management strategy to keep the crowd informed on existing defects and your defect management protocols keep such counts under control. But then again, you want your crowd to be as independent as possible from your core internal processes to empower it work at its creative best. This is thus a tough call to make in reality, which you will master with experience and the right understanding of your crowd's background. There is one study that analyzed this problem and summarized that five testers each with 2 hours of testing time reported 71% more defects than one tester testing for 9.8 hours. The study also showed the high count of duplicate and invalid bugs from a group of 130 students that were brought in for testing (as seen in Figure 6.2), highlighting the importance of and need for a thought-through defect management strategy in engaging with a large crowd.

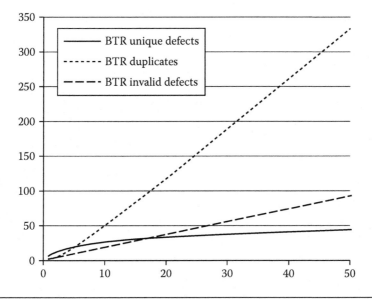

Figure 6.2 Relationship of crowd size and defects.

7

WIN YOUR TEAM'S SUPPORT IN IMPLEMENTING CROWDSOURCED TESTING

People who work together will win, whether it be against complex football defences, or the problems of modern society.

—Vince Lombardi[20]

Nothing can really be achieved without support of and buy-in from the team. A stakeholder team is a group that impacts or is impacted by the activities of a given project. The core product team is often a part of the stakeholder group, but in addition, the senior management, executive management, and users may also be part of the stakeholder group. Since, for our discussion here, the team is also part of the stakeholder community, we will mainly look at winning the team and project sponsors' support. Anytime anything external to the team is brought in, there is always resistance. It is important to see this resistance in a healthy spirit, so as to promote discussions around what is right for the project and determine implementation practices that will best meet the project's specific needs. Crowdsourced testing is no exception to this belief, where organizations have and continue to face resistance for bringing in the external crowd at varied levels. And unless the team driving the crowdsourced testing effort works on understanding where the resistance is originating from, what the resistance or concern areas are, it will not be able to work on solutions. So, as the first step, start identifying the concerns, do your home-work on what the solutions need to be, try out a few solutions on the ground, ensure you have addressed all concerns, and then meet the stakeholders on an ongoing basis to ensure you are in sync with them. While at a high level, stakeholder concerns on crowdsourced testing are very similar to the challenges of crowdsourced testing that we discussed earlier, it is worth looking at them again at this time to ensure our solutions map to the identified concerns.

Even before we look at what their concerns are, let's look at the definition of a stakeholder and see who all fits in this group. As mentioned at the start of this chapter, a stakeholder is someone who impacts or is impacted by a project's tasks. He could include:[21]

1. Internal entities:
   a. Your core execution team—aka project team
   b. Your project sponsors, including your immediate management and senior/executive management
   c. Other groups in your organization that are interested or have a vested interest in your project
2. External entities:
   a. Shareholders
   b. End users
   c. Suppliers
   d. Community at large
   e. Government
   f. Social groups (nonprofit organizations)

Of this set, not all of them might be relevant stakeholders that you need to care about in your current project. Identifying the set that you need to care about is important, and once that happens, you are not only going to work on winning their support for this project, but are mainly going to work on winning their trust for the concept of crowdsourced testing as a whole.

Even before we look at winning stakeholder's support specific to crowdsourced testing, at a generic level, how would you go about this process, especially in the current-day world where time and resources are often limited? Jo Ann Sweeney[22] has written a nice post on this, basing her model on Bill Quirke's theory and book, *The Communications Escalator* (Figure 7.1).

This model talks about working with stakeholders all the way from creating awareness to helping them understand the situation at hand, winning their support, getting them involved, and reaching the final stage of getting their full-fledged commitment for your project. With this initial understanding, if you read through the rest of the chapter, you will be able to understand why stakeholders might resist to your

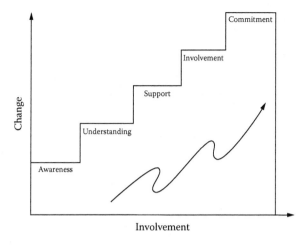

Figure 7.1   The communications escalator in working your way up with stakeholders.

crowdsourced testing effort, and how you can build a step-by-step process to ultimately win their commitment.

At a very broad level, their concerns are around the implementation aspects (including the overhead and security) and the softer aspects of team motivation. More specifically, stakeholder's concerns are around:

1. **The additional value that the crowd is said to bring in—** especially when they have heavily invested in a core team internally and possibly an outsourced test team too: This is more so the case when the team brings in the crowd just to supplement the internal testing team's bandwidth.

2. **Additional management overhead to be expended on this effort:** This is a valid concern that we have already discussed and also considered how to address, in our earlier section on crowdsourced testing challenges and implementation. This is an important point to consider in planning a crowdsourced test effort, as it is not a "throw over the fence and the work will get done" situation. It needs careful planning and implementation efforts from the internal team.

3. **Product's intellectual property (IP), confidentiality, privacy, and antipiracy requirements:** This is typically the major cause of concern for stakeholders, as they fear that bringing in external entities will impact the product's privacy

requirements and eat into the confidentiality requirements, especially when they have no control over the crowd that tests the product. This is especially true in the case of larger crowd efforts involving the public at large (public beta), where there could even be competitors spying to see what your offerings are. We looked at this from an earlier challenge and a solution standpoint, but you cannot overlook this when working with your stakeholders. Also, they have concerns around piracy. What if the crowd takes a commercial license to test the software but unethically continues to use it for its needs after the testing time frame? Have you thought about activation periods to ensure licenses are valid only for the required periods of time?

4. **Adverse impact on the internal team's motivation levels:** If the right level of understanding is not established, one of the more serious repercussions of engaging the crowd is a de-motivated internal team. This de-motivation stems from the insecurity and sense of threat that their roles are in danger due to the crowd involvement. This could lead not just to team de-motivation, but also to team attrition. This is enough cause for concern for stakeholders, as they do not want to do anything that would impact their core internal team and the stability therein. So, even if they know that this can be worked around, it takes a lot of convincing to show the value of crowd testing that they are willing to take the extra effort to engage with the testers and work toward a peaceful balance between the internal testing team and the crowd testing team.

5. **The guarantee of the quality of test effort?** Will crowd testing not randomize the overall test findings and requirements of the test strategy? This is yet another concern we already talked about earlier. There is truth to this, where, unless planned for effectively, the crowd's test efforts and results can randomize the internal test management, leading to more chaos than the value they derive. This is a striking concern for stakeholders, as they do not want this randomization impacting the product's overall quality and sign-off schedule. Also, the internal team has been carefully trained along the quality

requirements of this specific organization. How it can expect the same level of quality from an external crowd that it has no have control over is one of its core concerns.

You may realize that most of these concerns are ones that we already discussed earlier on. And if so, the solutions were also discussed as part of Chapter 5, when we talked about implementing crowdsourced testing. If so, can we not leverage the same in winning the team's support and the stakeholder's support? Let's address this from two angles. How do I work on winning my core team's support and then the stakeholders' (in this case, the project sponsors and executive management's support)? This needs to be a methodical process taken up step-by-step, which is what we will discuss in the next two sections:

Winning the product team's support: As a product team, you have diverse roles, including the business team, the marketing team, the design team, the development team, the test team, and the build and operations team, to name some of the core ones. The team that is probably impacted the most by getting the crowd to test is the test team. It will need to collaborate with the crowd testers in a sense that it does not directly talk to them, but will have to see what areas are assigned to the two teams to ensure there isn't duplication (in some areas alone, a planned duplication may be accounted for to bring in extra test coverage), see how defect management is being handled, and help the development with any defects filed by the crowd where extra troubleshooting and debugging may be needed. So, the test team incurs a lot more overhead in engaging with the crowd than anyone else. They are also the ones who are more confused about the delineation in roles between theirs and the crowd, creating a sense of insecurity about their jobs, now that an external entity is at play. So first, the team driving the crowdsourced test effort and the test management team will have to very clearly explain to the test team the following points:

1. Crowdsourced testing is a supplemental effort to the core testing effort. It is not a stand-alone effort that will replace internal testing.

2. There are specific areas, such as the ones we discussed earlier on around what not to crowd test, that make it clear that such areas are core specializations of the formal test team. Areas where the crowd is leveraged to test are largely not going to eat into the formal test team's piece of the pie.

3. The crowd is often brought in for its end user experience or domain skills (including specific language skills), and sometimes to augment an internal test team's bandwidth.

When the test management team takes the time to explain these to the formal test team, its sense of insecurity and feeling threatened goes down. Rather, it emerges with a sense of empowerment to ensure it extend its support to the crowd team in possible ways to help improve the quality of the product under test.

Similarly, while extra overhead from a crowd testing effort cannot be avoided, as long as the team understands that additional bandwidth will be set aside, for specific people to drive this effort, and it is made to see the benefits of bringing in the crowd, the team's concerns can be easily alleviated. But as in most solutions, this is not a one-time effort. On an ongoing basis the team needs to be involved in understanding any new concerns, how the model is working out, and determine any newer solutions that are needed.

Winning the project sponsors' support: We already looked at the concerns that project sponsors typically have, and that a planned step-by-step process is needed in winning their support. The flow shown in Figure 7.2 is a good approach in winning project sponsors' support, which can then be mildly customized as required to meet an individual team's needs.

As we look through each of them, in greater detail:

1. **Identify stakeholders, prioritize them, and engage early:** Who constitutes the stakeholder group varies from one company to another, from one team to another within the same company and even between releases in the same team. So, as a first step, identify your stakeholders specific to the project at hand. Clearly winning

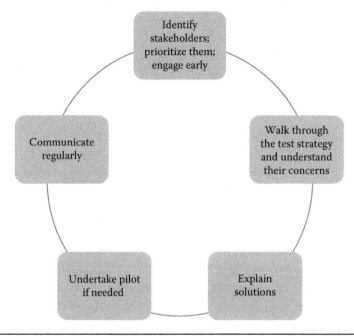

Figure 7.2 Winning your stakeholders' support to crowdsource your testing effort.

everyone's support may not always be possible. Prioritize your stakeholders and determine whose support matters the most for your project at this given time so you know where to expend your efforts. Also, engaging early on is important. At this stage quality goals are still being established. This will give you an opportunity to hear their concerns early on and address them in your quality strategy, rather than involving them much later in the game when changes are more difficult to make and expensive to manage.

2. **Walk through the test strategy and understand their concerns:** At this stage, do not assume that your project sponsors know what crowdsourced testing is. They probably have a very narrow view and understanding of it, which is why there are probably concerned. Explain all manifestations of crowdsourced testing, which one you plan to use, and how it will benefit your project. As you do this, very carefully observe and make note of what their concerns are specific to crowdsourced testing, which will help

you build your solution to address them. Acknowledge the concerns they describe and explain to them that this will be a supplement to the core testing effort.

3. **Explain solutions:** Tell them that you have built this as an educated model. You have thought through which model of crowdsourced testing will work for your project, the what, when, and how of crowdsourced testing, along with learnings from past success and failure stories. This will give them the confidence that you have done your homework, and that you are not jumping into it based on the market hype for the model. Present the checks and balances you have put together to ensure neutrality in adopting the model, explain that you have carefully analyzed all their concerns, and ensure there are mapping solutions to alleviate them. Present the one-to-one or one-to-many mapping to show that every concern of theirs will be mitigated by one or more solutions, which will help them not only feel more secure, but also gradually start seeing the value of crowdsourced testing.

4. **Undertake a pilot if needed:** While it is understandable that crowdsourced testing in itself demands extra efforts, and that doing a pilot is only going to add more overhead up front, the value from it often surpasses the effort put in. A pilot very strongly helps in two ways. It is an implemented proof for the stakeholders that this model will work for their project, along with seeing how the effort will work on a larger scale, and that their concerns have been taken care of. Additionally, it is a tremendous dose of positive boost for the person or team driving the crowdsourced testing, that the model will work on the project and that they are taking the right step forward. This will give them practical input on what went well, where more focus is needed, what can be done better, areas to watch for, etc., to keep in mind for a larger effort, helping them get into it with more confidence, data, and experience. So, agreed it is additional effort up front, but it often goes a long way in implementing a successful longer-term crowdsourced testing engagement.

5. **Ongoing communication:** Sometimes, teams take care of all the due diligence explained above, up front, but miss the element of ongoing communication once they get busy with their project routines and tasks. They may have accounted for ongoing communication but are just so preoccupied that they are unable to take care of it. The test management team and, again, the person driving the crowdsourced testing effort should definitely watch for this and ensure this does not happen. It is important to be in touch with the sponsors on a regular basis, stick to the predefined communication protocols (yet flexibly making changes on the go based on what you see on the ground), and keep them informed of the good, bad, and ugly of the crowdsourced testing effort. Also, do not assume that your stakeholders identified earlier on are still the same set of people you need to track. Stakeholders often change, and the newer set of people may have a completely different set of priorities, concerns, and wants and may not align with what you identified early on. This is inevitable in project management, and it is in your and your crowdsourced testing effort's best interest for you to stay on top of your current set of stakeholders on an ongoing basis.

One may be an expert in project management, including global team management of both geographically distributed teams and an outsourced team that you are working with. However, a crowdsourced test effort is a ball game of its own. You are dealing with an external entity with whom you may not have interacted, you do not have any formal agreement with, and whose interest levels in your project may be short-lived if it is not adequately motivated and challenged. At the same time, you have internal challenges to handle, dealing with your own product team and stakeholders, as we saw above. One may even wonder, given all these complexities at hand, if it is even worth taking up a crowdsourced testing effort. As we have seen in several of the past chapters, the value of crowdsourced testing is enormous. It is a need of the day in most product development efforts. If you carefully weigh your returns to the challenges at hand, you will be able to determine whether crowdsourced testing makes sense for your project or not. In most cases, the question is not really about whether it makes sense—it is more about where and when it does make sense. Choose the right person to drive the crowdsourced testing in your team, who is able to take on this objective analysis and take back his findings to the decision makers in building a custom crowdsourced testing effort that your team will benefit from. This is a person who not only understands the product, the technology, and can handle the crowd's product queries, but more importantly, a person with core traits around successful people management (including working through the expectations of various entities at various levels, including the executive management team), communication, and who can instill a positive work culture between the internal team and the crowd. Once such a person or a team is identified, you are well on your way to succeeding in your crowdsourced testing effort, not only from a core implementation angle, but also from the team support and empowerment angles, to make this project a reality and success. This is a person who understands that without the support of stakeholders, crowdsourced testing will fail even in areas where it can otherwise succeed. Thus, this person assumes the role of a crowdsourced testing leader to make this project happen with the support of stakeholders and at the end of the day. This is a person who, as summarized by Napoleon Bonaparte, is "a Leader who is a Dealer in Hope."[47]

Did You Know?[D-9]

We have seen in Chapter 5 when to use crowdsourced testing, where to use it, and how to carefully implement it. The same points extend to the larger umbrella of crowdsourcing too. While crowdsourcing continues to be an educated decision that not all stakeholders immediately buy in to, we are seeing increasing examples of how organizations are using crowdsourcing for a range of activities that would have been very tightly coupled to the internal teams even a few years back. Here's one such example of how General Mills is using crowdsourcing for myriad activities:

General Mills has created the General Mills Worldwide Innovation Network (G-WIN) to aggressively get innovative and creative ideas from the crowdsourced community across its range of products. Such a plan encompasses ideas for:

1. New products that align with the General Mills brand
2. Packaging of existing and new products
3. Enhancements to manufacturing, service, or marketing processes
4. Ingredient recommendations for food products
5. Technology recommendations for General Mills IT processes
6. Ideas for improving the organization's digital efficiencies and performance

The G-WIN open call is fairly open in that anyone can get to the website and submit their suggestions via the "Submit a Novel Proposal" link. If this is the kind of feedback the company is eliciting from the community at large, one can imagine the tremendous support it must have from the internal stakeholders in this initiative.

8

LET'S UNDERSTAND CROWDSOURCED TESTING HOLISTICALLY

And in the absence of facts, myth rushes in, the kudzu of history.

—**Stacy Schiff**[23]
Cleopatra: A Life[24]

Myths, which are beliefs or ideas often considered to be false, are omnipresent. They exist in every subject area or discipline; software testing and specifically crowdsourced testing are no exceptions. Since external entities are often involved in crowdsourced testing, the concept is still new and is in its naïve implementation stages, and the industry and the user base at large hold a lot of myths on this subject. These will continue to exist until the subject on crowdsourced testing gains maturity and gets industry-wide acceptance. To be able to reach such a state, ongoing practice and implementation in possible ways and forms within projects are important. As someone who has read through the last seven chapters of this book, this is an important chapter for you from two aspects:

1. Understand myths related to every chapter from the standpoint of differentiating what is a myth and what is a fact. By now, you would be able to do this yourself given the understanding of crowdsourced testing you have built. As we do this, we will also briefly summarize every chapter in about two to three sentences, which will help you refresh the entire book's reading through these short synopses.

2. Understand what career options exist for a tester or, for that matter, anyone who is a user or a domain expert who wants to spend their time and effort in testing a product the crowdsourced way.

Chapter 1: Introducing the Crowd

The core of this chapter was to introduce you to who forms the crowd, with the message that the crowd is not a new phenomenon. It has existed for a long time, and so has the concept of crowdsourcing. It is just that it has gotten a lot of attention in recent years, since it was officially baptized, helping it gain status as an industry-recognized terminology.

> **Myth 1:** As crowdsourcing is widely used these days even by software companies, only people in the software industry can be part of the crowd.
>
> **Facts:** While it is true that people from the software industry can also be part of a crowd, it is a complete myth that only they can be part of the crowd. The very fact that you engage the crowd because of its end user mind-set, questioning nature, analytical skills, or subject matter expertise makes anyone from the community at large a target candidate to participate in crowdsourcing. It is true that in crowdsourced development, programming knowledge is often inevitable, but it is far from truth that for crowdsourcing at large you need to be part of the software industry.

Chapter 2: An Overview into Crowdsourcing

In this chapter, we took a big leap in helping you understand what is crowdsourcing, what the various forms of crowdsourcing are, what is crowdsourced testing, and where it fits in to the crowdsourcing umbrella along with a lot of examples. We talked about how crowdsourcing has a very simple meaning, yet is very powerful, and that it can span across company types (products, services), scales, technologies, domains, and can be done even internal to an organization, as long as you understand your crowd's motivating factors, to be associated with you. One common myth the industry holds is that crowdsourcing and outsourcing are one and the same. We looked at this elaborately, covering both areas of similarities and differences, helping you get a full picture of the two. So we will look at another myth here from the standpoint of crowdsourced testing's definition.

Myth 2: Crowdsourced testing can be done *only* through formal business models and organizations that provide crowdsourced testing services.

Facts: The model defined in this myth is also a valid form of crowdsourced testing. Let us take our own case. At QA InfoTech, we have a formal practice around crowdsourced testing, and any external user can come register with us to take on crowdsourced testing. The myth here is around the use of the word *only*. You need to understand that this is not the only form in which crowdsourced testing can be implemented. It can be successfully arranged by an organization that is inviting end users for crowd testing wherein they directly interact with the crowd without involving any interim entities. The crowd test team can be internal to the organization or can be an end user base or a team of domain experts, where the organization believes in a simple fact that crowdsourced testing is bringing in the community at large to test your product and provide feedback. That said, when you reach out to organizations that provide crowdsourced testing as a service, especially to connect with the community, the process may be simpler, as they already have a platform to take on crowdsourced testing and have a database of crowd users that they can connect with quickly.

Chapter 3: Why Leverage the Crowd for Software Testing?

In this chapter we started looking closely at software quality assurance and testing, understanding where software quality stands today and why we specifically need additional solutions like crowdsourced testing in the current day. We also looked at each and every test area to see where crowdsourced testing is more feasible and successful than in other areas, helping us understand that crowdsourced testing is not applicable for all test areas or types.

Myth 3: Crowdsourcing is possible only in software testing and not in software development.

Fact: This is not true. Crowdsourcing is equally possible in software development as in software testing. Linux is a living testimony of crowdsourced development. Similarly, topcoder.com has several examples of crowdsourced development projects that hit the market periodically. Also, all of the best practices we have discussed earlier for implementing a crowdsourced testing project are equally applicable for crowdsourced development too. That said, it is true that crowdsourcing is easier and more valuable for crowdsourced testing than for development because the crowd in case of testing need not have programming knowledge and is often brought in because of this end user representation, domain expertise, or testing skills. So, there is a larger pool of people to choose from in the case of crowdsourced testing compared to crowdsourced development.

Chapter 4: Is Crowdsourced Testing a No-Brainer Solution to All Quality Problems?

In this chapter we introduced the ground reality around crowdsourced testing. We talked about how although the model has great benefits and value to bring to the table, it is not a one-stop solution to all quality problems, and that it is not even often a stand-alone testing solution. It is a supplemental solution that is to be leveraged alongside core testing or formal testing techniques. We also talked about crowdsourced testing challenges and limitations primarily from security, implementation, overhead, and stakeholder buy-in standpoints, also touching upon what areas should not be considered for crowdsourced testing.

> **Myth 4:** The internal test team's position is often threatened by engaging a crowdsourced testing team.
>
> **Fact:** Like in the past, when the industry was new to outsourcing, a common belief now is that if crowdsourced testers gain entry into a testing group, they would slowly penetrate deep enough to threaten the positioning of the core internal test team. This is a complete myth, and there is no truth to it. In fact, if done the right way, the core test team can really be empowered to succeed in their roles as well as help the crowd test team succeed, creating a win-win situation for all entities as well as the product under test. The core team needs to understand that given the current need where end user feedback and testing on real devices, across geographies, Internet bandwidths, etc.,

are very valuable to the product and these are difficult to get done internally, a crowd adds tremendous value to a product's quality. They are only a supplemental team, and there are specific core testing areas that cannot be crowdsourced. When these are clarified internally, it helps get not only the test team's buy-in, but also the stakeholders' buy-in, increasing the chances of the crowdsourced test effort's success.

Chapter 5: How to Successfully Implement Crowdsourced Testing

This is a very important chapter in this book. It discusses in detail, along with examples, how crowdsourced testing needs to be a formally planned test effort, an educated decision driven by best practices around what, when, and how to crowdsource in your testing. It asks you to keep in mind that over and above the set defined in this book, customization to one's own project needs is important. We covered examples from various disciplines, domains, and scenarios, helping you understand the practical implementations of crowdsourced testing.

Myth 5: The management overhead in implementing a crowdsourced testing effort is quite high.

Facts: This is partially true and partially false. It is a fact that there is considerable management overhead in a crowdsourced project, not necessarily crowdsourced testing. One cannot throw the project off the fence to a group of crowd testers and expect it to be done on time and comprehensively. There is a need for an internal person or a team to drive the crowdsourced testing effort. However, keep in mind that this is true of any global project in the current-day world and is not new to crowdsourcing alone. Also, the crowd is a smart set of people, usually end users, testers, or domain experts who do not want to be handheld or micromanaged. They just need core guidelines, beyond which they need the independence to bring out their best. Also, the management effort may seem chaotic if it has not been planned well. So, keep in mind that while crowdsourced testing does need additional management cycles internally, it is not prohibitive enough to the model itself. The value from crowdsourced testing often exceeds the overhead factor that it is in the team's best interest to plan the implementation effort well and keep it under control to maintain the team's sanity.

Chapter 6: Defect Management in Crowdsourced Testing

Given the importance of defect management in any software project, we decided to dedicate one whole chapter to this subject. Herein we touched on defect management practices in general, how it applies to crowdsourced testing, what best practices from generic defect management can be leveraged here, and real-life case studies of how defect management was handled. We discussed the entire chapter through a series of questions with the intent of foreseeing what questions you might have and our responses for them.

> **Myth 6:** Since it is ideal to maintain independence in the crowd for the team to succeed, defects filed by other crowd testers or by the internal team should not be exposed to the crowd.

> **Facts:** This may or may not be a myth because this is totally the choice of the team that is driving the crowd test effort. Some teams prefer to retain independence among the crowd to reduce communication bandwidth as well as maximize their creativity, not letting them talk to other crowd testers. In such cases they may decide to not show them the list of bugs filed by other testers in the spirit of maintaining total confidentiality in the crowd's output. On the other hand, to reduce the overall management overhead, resolve queries, help the crowd maximize their output, and minimize duplicate bugs, some teams may resort to complete transparency, where the crowd gets to see the defects filed by everyone else. Some teams may settle halfway in between, releasing a list of known issues from time to time, to bring everyone in sync on product status; however, they may decide not to divulge who filed the defects. There is no right or wrong answer here, and it totally depends on the team's comfort level and product needs, to decide which route to take. However, in practice, in most public betas the first approach of total independence is typically adopted. In private betas where the company works with a selected or even an internal crowd, the second

approach of total transparency may be adopted. In public betas, sometimes the third approach of selective transparency (through discussion groups, forums) may also be taken up. So, decide what works for you based on your needs, keeping in mind your end goal of helping the crowd, your team, and your product succeed in finding as many defects as possible before the product's release.

Chapter 7: Win Your Team's Support in Implementing Crowdsourced Testing

Any effort that is undertaken in an organization needs the buy-in of all entities involved, whether this means the immediate team working on the project or the executive sponsors who are making the case for the project's existence. Specific to crowdsourcing, there is the belief that getting stakeholder buy-in is very difficult, if not impossible. While there is some truth to this, it is often justified by specific concerns that the stakeholders have. If the team working on crowdsourcing assignments does its due diligence to understand stakeholder concerns and methodically addresses them, it is not only possible to win their support, but also maximize the overall chances of the project succeeding. With this crux that was discussed in this chaper, let's look at a myth specific to this message.

> **Myth 7:** Even if they buy in, stakeholders are very conservative in the areas where they allow crowdsourcing to happen.
>
> **Fact 7:** Every stakeholder is different. The level to which they want to take on crowdsourcing really depends on how conservative or open they are, what their risk-taking mind-sets are, what their specific markets and user demands are, etc. However, this statement is turning out to be more of a myth by the day. The kinds of activities for which crowdsourcing is being considered a viable option are making the case very strong for a bright future for this discipline. In the "Did You Know" section of Chapter 7, we looked at some of the diverse areas General Mills is using crowdsourcing for. That was just one example. There are many organizations out there that are embracing the crowd for a varied set of activities that a few years back were very closed and internal to

the organization. With the due diligence on protecting their intellectual property (IP), the creative solutions and applications from crowdsourcing are reaching never before seen heights, and this is just a start to seeing more such solutions emerge in the coming years.

Chapter 8: Let's Understand Crowdsourced Testing Holistically

In the current chapter, as we look at myths and facts on crowdsourced testing from across chapters, one other important area that we are also going to look at is how one can build a successful career in crowdsourced testing. While there will be several of you who are interested in this topic, there is one myth that is important to understand from both a company (crowd seeker) and an individual (crowd tester) standpoint:

Myth 8: Putting together a crowd test team is very easy. It can be done at the last minute, as and when the need arises.

Fact: There is hardly any truth to this. In fact, selecting the right crowd test team is the first step in being able to succeed in crowdsourced testing. Since there is no formal agreement with the crowd, except for a nondisclosure agreement in some cases, bringing in the right crowd and motivating its members to sustain them on the project is a very challenging task. The person driving the crowd testing effort needs to be a good people manager to accomplish this. Similarly, the crowd tester cannot assume that he can be on-boarded into a crowd test project on the fly. In most cases, the organization may have an informal discussion or interview to ensure you are the right crowd candidate it is looking for. This process may take some time, and similar to a regular job interview, the organization may have a number of registered crowd testers and may only have a few people that it is looking for in each geography, age group, background, etc. So, do not assume that the process will be quick and you have a sure shot at being selected. Also, not all crowd testing initiatives are done effectively and diligently from an implementation standpoint. Thus, whether you are a crowd tester seeker or a crowd tester, take the time to find the right match and build a database up front so you are prepared when the need actually arises to either work with the right crowd pool or work for the right organization.

Additional Myths and Facts

Without elaborating a whole lot, let us look at a few more myths in the industry on crowdsourcing. We have covered some of these in our discussion above in greater detail.

1. **Quality is in danger when dealing with crowdsourcing** (more from a crowd development angle). This is a myth to the extent that when done in a planned and thought-through manner, with solid implementation, crowdsourcing can be successful for both development and testing. Also refer to myths 3 and 5 for more details.

2. **Crowdsourcing testing brings down the total cost of quality.** This is partially true, as crowdsourced testing helps expand the test coverage and user reach before product release. However, as discussed throughout the book, the right practices need to be in place to leverage the wisdom of the crowd, failing which this effort will increase the total project cost rather than bring down the total cost of quality.

3. **Too many cooks spoil the broth.** We all know this is a very commonly used quote. However, does this apply to crowdsourcing where we are intentionally bringing in too many cooks? We have seen the value of crowdsourcing, whether it is development or testing. Keep in mind, with the right checks and balances, this quote can be defied even in the culinary discipline. So, given the value that crowdsourcing can potentially bring to the table, this is certainly a myth in the field of software development, if the right practices are employed.

At the end of this section, let's understand holistically that the value or return on investment from crowdsourcing, specifically crowdsourced testing, is tremendous. However, it can take a completely tangential turn if planning and implementation are poor. It thus takes the team's buy-in, commitment, trust, solid planning, and implementation, all of which together can take the potential of crowdsourced testing to unimaginable heights. With this understanding, let us move on the next section on building a solid and viable career in crowdsourced testing to help you take back additional actionable items from this book.

Is Crowdsourced Testing a Viable Career to Build?

The world is full of willing people; some willing to work, the rest willing to let them.[48]

—Robert Frost
American poet, 1874–1963

In the last few years a lot of organizations have been reaching out to the crowd, be it internal or external, in bringing the value of crowdsourced testing to enhance product quality. Crowdsourced testing platforms are being built to provide a formal medium through which testers can test, making it more viable to reach out to the remote crowd. A tester sitting at home in India is now able to test remotely for an application that is being built in the United States, without any need for an office space, a visa, a formal agreement with the company, etc. The implementation model of crowdsourced testing has thus eliminated several barriers that might exist in leveraging global knowledge in testing a product. While the feasibility continues to grow over years, the tester also needs to keep in mind that there are quite a few differences between building a formal testing career and a crowdsourced testing career. At a high level, see Table 8.1.

Who Can Become a Crowdsourced Tester?

In Chapter 1 we touched elaborately upon traits that make a person a crowdsourced tester, speaking about end user mind-set, subject matter expertise, and the testing attitude. Essentially, as a crowd tester you can add value to a product's test effort if you are or potentially are the product's end user, have subject matter expertise or domain expertise specific to the product under test, or are a software tester who has free bandwidth or cycles that you can devote to crowdsourced testing.

So, theoretically, a developer or a designer or a build engineer could become a crowd tester as long as he or she has the inclination for it, and as a person that has a testing mind-set—more of a questioning

Table 8.1 Formal vs. Crowdsourced Testing Career

PARAMETER	FORMAL TESTING CAREER	CROWDSOURCED TESTING CAREER
Number of jobs	Typically one, unless you are consulting with multiple companies with the consent of all companies to work at multiple places.	Can be many. You can register to be a crowd tester with several groups or organizations and there is typically no stopping from a conflict of interest standpoint, unless you have signed an nondisclosure agreement (NDA) that prevents you from working on similar applications/products.
Variety in work	Variety between projects is limited. Typically a tester is tied to one project for a given release.	Variety between projects is high. It is up to the tester to sign up for as many crowd test events as he can manage.
Duration in work	Long term in nature and tied to the release the tester is working on.	Crowd tester is often brought into the project only at specific times when the project is ready for the crowd's eyes. So, the overall crowd testing duration may only last a few days or weeks, unless the crowd is a private crowd where its members engage as subject matter experts (SMEs) from the start of the project.
Duration between projects	A core testing team member has activities lined up throughout the year to ensure there are no breaks in his work schedule, as the company is paying him a regular salary. In case of contractors, the assignment may end after a project release and may commence only at the start of the next project.	Since the crowd tester works on projects only at specific times when it makes sense to bring in a crowd, duration between projects is often high. Also, the company engaging the crowd is under no financial binding to engage the crowd tester through the year. However, if the team is a very trusted crowd that the company does not want to let go of, it may look at assigning interim tasks to engage the crowd on an ongoing basis.
Randomization	Internal randomization is often high due to the agile nature of projects and the need for cross-collaboration.	External randomization is high, working on multiple projects, communicating remotely, working with a crowd project liaison who the tester has not met.
Kind of testing tasks	More variety in testing tasks, including challenging and strategic ones such as test automation, performance testing, and metrics management, to name some.	Not much variety in testing tasks, although variety comes in from multiple projects and companies that the crowd tester may be engaged with. Tasks are typically centric on End to End (E2E), functional, performance, compatibility, and localization tests. However, the crowd has a high excitement level given that it is actually using the product or application like how an end user would.
Transparency and independence in work	Full transparency at work with visibility into what other testers are working on, defects filed on the project, and ability to communicate with anyone on the team to get the work done.	Most often transparency is restricted to the level of communication that the crowd liaison has with the tester. Companies prefer the crowd tester to work in isolation to bring out his best, keeping him independent of other crowd testers.

mind-set with good analytical skills and observation, the crowd tester can add significant value to the project under test. Similarly, a math professor could be a crowd tester of an educational software that is being developed. As an online shopper, one could be a crowd tester of an e-commerce web application. As an avid mobile user, one could be a crowd tester of a mobile application. As a gamer, one could be a crowd tester of a new game. As a tester who took a professional break for about 5 years, one could look at reentering the industry by becoming a crowd tester. As a student, one could gain some direct project experience by signing up to be a crowd tester. The options are really limitless, and anyone can become a crowd tester as long as they have the end user, subject matter, or test skills and are willing to perform a dedicated task to help improve the product's quality, as well as hone their testing skills.

What Should I Do to Prepare and Be Successful in Crowdsourced Testing Assignments?

While we discussed in the previous section that anyone with skills around being an end user, subject matter expert, or tester can potentially become a crowdsourced tester, not everyone is successful at it. Here's a basic list of what one can do to prepare to become a crowdsourced tester and how to pave one's path to success:

Decide how much time you can dedicate for crowdsourced testing: In most cases, crowdsourced testing is taken up by people who already have a full-time day job. They may be doing this out of their interest, desire to use their testing skills or learn something new, loyalty to a certain brand, or wanting to get back into their career after a break/potentially switch jobs. So, one may not have the luxury of working on crowd testing assignments full-time. As a first step, decide how much time you can set aside for crowdsourced testing. There is no right or wrong number here to be successful. It is your call based on your interest, availability, and other priorities at hand.

Research to register at the right places: In recent times, there are ample crowdsourced testing platforms. Several companies are attempting to take on crowdsourced testing. Do your homework online to identify places that suit your skill set and interests.

Pick a couple of trustworthy places that you want to stick with: Although one can potentially work with more than one crowdsourced testing seeker, it would be very randomizing to work with multiple places. So, from your researched list, pick a few that best meet your needs and profile. Pick ones where there is maximum usage of your skills, because the more you can showcase, the better will be your chances of success.

Revisit your devices inventory: One of the reasons companies or groups are attempting to connect with crowd testers is to leverage the devices they have—especially mobile devices, including smartphones, tablets, and e-readers, ranging across various operating system (OS) SKUs, device makers, Internet bandwidths, locale settings, etc. Some of your old and obsolete devices may also be very valuable for them from a backward compatibility angle. So, make sure as you revisit your resume specific to crowdsourced testing, you have revisited your devices inventory and updated them in your profile.

Practice your language skills: Language skills, especially written, are one of the major reasons companies reach out to crowdsourced testers. This helps them verify content and also get translations done from the experts directly. So, refresh your list on the languages you know and also refresh your proficiency in them, if it has been some time since you used them.

Think through your domain specialties: Domain space is a huge real estate to operate within. You may have a background in sciences, math, arts, computer, and Internet technology. You may have been a banker in your yester years but have now moved out of banking and probably into insurance software testing. Think through your current and past domain skills and honestly rate yourself on them. Practice and refresh your domain skills specific to the project you are considering for crowdsourced testing, especially around workflows. This is not from a standpoint of preparing for an interview or an exam, but to help you do a realistic job, if you decide to take this route.

Build your crowdsourced testing resume showcasing your diversity: Building one's resume is very important to enable anyone to understand your potential. This is all the more important in crowdsourced testing since the organization, person, or group that is engaging you will most often not meet you in person. So, what you call out in your resume will need to do a lot of the selling for who you are. While you need to be genuine in what you say, do not feel shy to quote even some seemingly minor details, because crowdsourced testing is all about diversity. Mention any past crowdsourced testing experience you have, any community project that you have worked on, any references you can provide, etc. Remember, this resume is going to be different from one that you use for a regular testing job. So, think through to ensure you have talked about yourself comprehensively, precisely, and professionally. This will help you go a long way in getting the right crowdsourced testing assignment. Look for sample crowdsourced testing resumes online, or bring this up in crowdsourcing forums to also get live input from others who have been involved in this space, in addition to the list we have provided above.

Look for some beta testing projects online to practice your testing skills: If you want to first try your shot at crowdsourced testing to determine your interest and scalability, look for any beta testing assignments from products or applications that you really like and try them out for a few days. This will give you the confidence you need and will also serve as a reality check on whether you are really cut out for this work. Furthermore, this could even be a nice addition on your crowdsourced testing resume.

Finalize your motivating factors: Not all crowd testing assignments may have money as the reward factor for the testers. In some cases, you may want to take part in a beta just because you really care for a certain brand and want to provide it your feedback. For examples, Gmail was in beta for a really long period of time, and people who gave it feedback were all crowd testers who did so based on their personal choice, not expecting any monetary return from Google.

So, if money is your main driver, make sure to pick choices accordingly. However, if you are not mainly looking at the money and are looking to build on your testing expertise and showcase this on your resume, then you will have more choices to work with. Again, there is no right or wrong answer here—pick what aligns with your needs and interests with the goal of sticking with it.

Talk to other crowdsourced testers in the community based on access: Crowdsourcing is a very community-driven phenomenon. See if you can meet with other crowdsourced testers in the community at forums, discussion boards, conferences, regular meeting groups, etc., based on people that align with your interest areas and domain. This will be a great networking exercise to help you build your crowdsourced testing options and expertise.

Maintain continuity in your effort unless you do not align with a specific company or group: If you like a certain project or a company for which you are a crowd tester, try and stick with it. Although you are not bound to stay with anyone in this space, the more you stick around, the better are your returns on investment, where your rating with the company goes up and you gain experience on its working style, product, needs, etc. This goes a long way in helping you and the organization be successful in the crowd testing assignment and shows well on your resume. So, arrive at the right balance of longevity versus variety to help you build a successful career in crowdsourced testing.

Obtain consent of your current organization, if required: If you are already a software tester, be sure to check with your current organization if it is OK to work as a crowdsourced tester. Since this is a freelance assignment of your own choice, it may be a conflict of interest to your current full-time job, and this is something you definitely need to check and ensure up front, to avoid any issues down the line. Sometimes this may even call for getting explicit written permissions from your organization, allowing you to partake in such crowdsourced testing assignments, and may also require you to periodically get such permissions for every new project you undertake. So, be sure to check with your organization to understand and clear constraints, if any.

Be on top on industry news: Outside of all the groundwork you have done in preparation to become a crowd tester, your dedication on the job, your socializing in the community, and staying current on industry news items are all very helpful in building a successful crowd testing career. Pick a couple of feeds that you want to read regularly for industry news to help you be up to date on events in the marketplace, competitor space, etc., that you can bring back into your testing effort. Crowdsourced testing is largely about end user representation. While you are an end user in most cases to start with, hone your end user representation even more by being current with what is happening in the community—this will go a long way in helping you succeed as a crowd tester.

Be dedicated in your task at hand: With all of the above groundwork you do, you also need to prove on the ground. Once you pick specific assignments to work on, give your best. Be responsive, define best practices around communication and work protocols for yourself, think out of box to find real end user issues, be creative in the work you do, and most importantly, be prompt. Develop your own discipline on the project and this will go a long way in building trust for yourself and help you increase your tester rating. Most crowdsourced tester seekers use weighted payment models, where they pay testers based on their ratings. Ratings are based on the work you do, your work ethics, longevity with the company, and several other factors that we discussed above. So if you like the work you do as a crowd tester for a certain company, be dedicated in your task to help you establish a successful stint in crowdsourced testing.

Although not a very formal practice as of yet, there are serious crowdsourced testers in the marketplace who make a living just through this activity. The potential is huge, as you have read through the chapters of this book so far. By now you should have been able to decide if crowdsourced testing will meet your needs, whether you are a company seeking crowd testers or an individual hoping to become a crowd tester. In the last 7–8 years, crowdsourcing is a trend that the information technology industry has been predicting and closely watching, whereas now is the time to delve deeper to look at crowdsourcing and crowdsourced testing trends in greater detail to see what it has in store over the next 3–5 years. This is precisely what we will look at over the two concluding chapters of this book.

Did You Know?[D-11,D-12]

Let's take a quick look back at some interesting events in the life cycle of crowdsourcing since its name was coined in 2006:

2006: The term *crowdsourcing*, a combination of *crowd* and *outsourcing*, was coined by Jeff Howe in a June 2006 article, "The Rise of Crowdsourcing."

2007: Dell initiated a website called IdeaStorm to generate ideas from the crowd. It has so far generated about 17,000 ideas and has implemented about 500 of them.

2008: Starbucks launched a similar site, MyStarbucksIdea.com, that has so far generated about 130,000 product ideas, including customer experience comments.

2009: Netflix announced a crowd contest to seek a solution for its recommendation engine algorithm and handed out a fat $1 million prize to the winners (a group of seven people). *AdAge* ran a crowd survey in which 61% surveyed commented that crowdsourcing was a threat to agencies and that crowdsourcing would fade out in a year. Given the growing use and popularity of crowdsourcing, it looks like the crowd can be wrong at times, after all, especially when it comes to predicting outcomes.

2010: Crowdsourcing was leveraged to address the Gulf of Mexico oil spill, where from over the 116,500 suggestions and engineering innovations that were received, 300 were considered for field testing and deployment; 20 of them were tested and immediately considered for implementation.

2011: The word *crowdsourcing* was included in the *Merriam Webster Collegiate Dictionary*.

2012: A report released in 2012 stated that in 2011 alone, $300 million was mobilized through crowdsourcing.

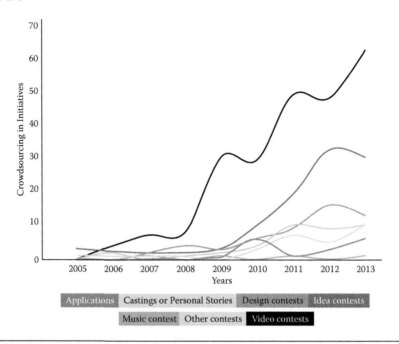

Figure 8.1   Varied applications of crowdsourcing since its inception.

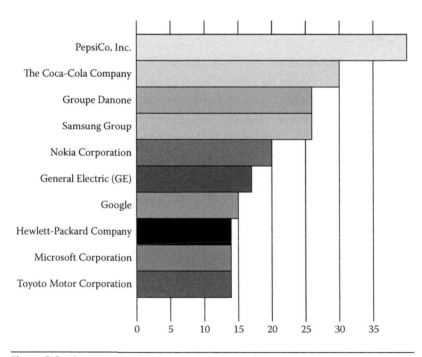

Figure 8.2   Companies that have been using crowdsourcing over the years.

2013: If we look at some of the best global brands (across industries), they used crowdsourcing only six times in 2006. This number had gone up to 131 in 2013.

2014: As of February 2014, the word *crowdsourcing* had 2,450,000 references on Google.

Figures 8.1 and 8.2 consist of interesting graphs showing what ways companies have used crowdsourcing the most and which companies have been using it the most since 2006.

9

FUTURE OF CROWDSOURCED TESTING

A journey of a thousand miles, begins with a single step.[49]

—Lao Tzu,
Chinese philosopher

The future of crowdsourcing is very promising, and its potential scope and reach are huge. However, to experience crowdsourcing and crowdsourced testing in one's own area of operations, you need to start small and take the first step. The content we have discussed over the course of this book will help you confidently take that first step toward successful crowdsourced testing. While understanding that concept and implementation specifics forms one major piece of the pie, it is equally important to keep track of the trends in a given discipline to be able to build an edge and better prepare for the upcoming requirements. At the time of writing this book, crowdsourcing and crowdsourced testing are upcoming areas that the information technology field is largely leveraging, and these are themselves trends as of today that the industry is closely watching. Over the course of this chapter, we will look at the current market size of the crowdsourcing industry, backed with some numbers, along with trends to watch for in crowdsourcing and crowdsourced testing.

Sizing the Crowdsourcing Industry

We discussed in earlier chapters how crowdsourcing has actually existed for centuries now; however, it got its official name and a lot more public visibility and recognition only after Jeff Howe called it as such, in 2006. So obviously, until then, although crowdsourcing was happening in pockets under various names, not much was done in terms of sizing the industry or predicting its future. Analysts have started tracking crowdsourcing in its various forms in these last few years, and the numbers they have released show a lot of promise for this industry.

Crowdsourcing, when taken up by organizations, referred to as enterprise crowdsourcing, has been showing amazing results in terms of revenue and number of crowdsourced workers. In 2009, the global market revenue was $140.8 million USD, which grew 52.5% to $214.9 million USD in 2010 and then to $375.7 million USD in 2011, booking a 74.7% growth over the previous year.

In terms of workers, the growth has been crossing the 100% mark year over year (YoY) from 1.34 million in 2009 to 3.10 million in 2010 to 6.29 million crowdsource workers in 2011.[25]

Massolution's report in 2012 has given quite some insight into how the crowdsourced industry is shaping up, including details such as:[26]

1. Crowdsourced worker count is increasing at more than 100% YoY.
2. Large enterprises with revenues upward of $1 billion USD are some of the early adopters of crowdsourced testing.
3. Crowdsourced workers work on crowd activities at least once a month, with more than half of them working on them at least once a day.
4. About 60% of crowd workers live in Europe or North America, and about 50% of them at least have a bachelor's degree, indicating that the awareness of crowdsourced testing is still restricted to the more literate and in developed nations.
5. More than 75% of the crowdsourced workers have another primary job on hand. This could mean that they are working on crowdsourced assignments for the following reasons:
   a. Some additional income
   b. Brand association for the organization they work for
   c. To build additional experience in newer areas and strengthen their overall profile/resume

Another set of interesting numbers/data points that showcase the power, potential, reach, and magnitude of crowdsourcing, especially in recent years, discusses the following, about the boom of crowd-sourcing in Asia:[27]

1. **A Chinese crowdsourcing site is the biggest employer in the world.** This company, Zhubajie, is into language crowd-sourcing and is said to have 7.6 million workers.

2. **Indian's crowdsourcing power users are said to earn 40 times more than that of an average American.** There are claims that these power users are actually entities and not individuals; however, they are said to earn more than $1 million USD per annum.

3. **Crowdsourcing in Asia is believed to have quadrupled.** Three of the five largest English-speaking populations globally are in Asia (India, Pakistan, and the Philippines). As factors that promote crowdsourcing, such as Internet penetration, go up in these nations, the reach of crowdsourcing will be even more in these geographies where people are looking for additional jobs and income.

4. **Enterprises are leveraging global talent by empowering global access.** U.S. crowdsourcing sites are launching local versions, such as Shutterstock and iStockPhoto, which recently launched Japanese, Chinese, and Korean versions of their sites. Similarly, Zhubajie has launched Witmart.com, an English version of its site, to allow U.S. enterprises access its 7.6 million Chinese workers.

These numbers clearly show the astounding growth of the crowd-sourcing industry, and additional numbers show even greater potential in specific areas of crowdsourcing, such as crowd funding, where in 2012 this market grew at 81%, raising $2.7 billion USD funding more than 1 million campaigns.[28]

Future of Crowdsourced Testing

Looking at the above numbers and the growth rates of crowdsourcing as a whole, the future is certainly bright. However, the growth will be cautiously optimistic, where it will not take over or replace existing sourcing methods. Rather, crowdsourcing and, in particular, crowdsourced testing will become a very strong supplemental option to the traditional sourcing methods for software testing. So let us understand some of the core trends we will witness from a crowdsourced testing angle. For ease of understanding, and to help with the holistic view, we will discuss the trends from four angles: market trends, end user trends, technology trends, and business trends of crowdsourced testing (see Table 9.1).

Market trends: Herein we will discuss trends around the crowd-sourcing test market, primarily involving the crowd testers and what changes they will see and experience in the next few years.

Business trends: Herein we will talk about the business, engagement models, and implementation process level trends in crowdsourced testing over the next few years.

Technology trends: In technology trends, we will look at what technology level impacts are in store for crowdsourced testing and what are the aiding technologies that will help grow this space.

Table 9.1 Trends in Crowdsourced Testing

MARKET TRENDS	BUSINESS TRENDS	TECHNOLOGY TRENDS	END USER TRENDS
• Number of crowd testers will continue to rise • Concept of a trusted and differentiated crowd will emerge — Expert sourcing • Better employment opportunities will shape up • Special interest groups will be formed • Newer groups, e.g., goverment will show interest in leveraging the crowd • Crowd testing will be valuable to strenthen student resumes	• Service level agreements at a soft level will be used • Internal buy in for crowdsourced testing will go up • Crowdsourced management team like vendor management teams will be built • Newer payment models will emerge • Crowdsourced testing will become a platform to find good full-time employees • Lot more legal scrutiny will be done	• Scope and reach of crowdsourced testing will increase manifold due to: • Enhanced Internet penetration • Growth in mobile technologies • Growth in social computing • Growth in cloud computing	• Crowdsourced testing will beef up end user product confidence and serve as a neutralizing agent in achieving desired quality • It will become an added certification on the product's richness and quality-enhancing market acceptance • End users will become more vocal to share their feedback (both positive and areas of improvement) with the product company

End user trends: This deals with trends around the end users of the product under development and how they will be impacted by crowdsourced testing.

Let's look at these trends in greater detail:

Market Trends

1. **The number of crowdsourced testers will increase.** There is increased awareness for crowdsourced testing both among the community (whether end users, testers, or domain experts) and among organizations that take on crowdsourced testing. This awareness is from various angles, including comfort, understanding, and implementation processes. This leads to more people in the community coming forward to perform crowdsourced testing, and this will only continue to go up in the coming years, helping the community better partake in the quality of products released.

2. **A concept of a trusted and differentiated crowd will emerge.** What we call expert sourcing is on the horizon. One limitation of the model we discussed in the earlier chapters was around the amateur crowd joining in along with the seasoned crowd, creating unwanted chaos among both the crowd community and the crowd management team. This pattern will change as organizations leverage the community for more and more crowdsourced testing projects where they would soon build a trusted crowd for themselves with whom they will be able to employ expert sourcing techniques.

3. **Better employment opportunities will shape up.** Crowdsourced testing will help generate better and increased employment opportunities, in terms of both quantity and quality. Organizations will reach out to the community not just for numbers, but more importantly, the skills they bring to the table, again going by the previous point where a trusted and differentiated crowd will emerge.

4. **Special interest groups will be formed.** Various social networks, especially the more popular ones like LinkedIn, already support special interest groups, helping connect people of similar

interests and skills. Such focused groups already help various professional activities, including finding people in the community with the right skills. This will continue to strengthen, with additional focus groups solely focusing on crowdsourced testing.

5. **Newer groups such as the government will show interest in crowdsourced testing.** Disciplines such as the government are usually very closed from a standpoint of information security, although they want to promote transparency among the community at large. As crowdsourced testing becomes more popular and the practices mature, alleviating some existing concerns around security, IP, etc., groups such as the government will also start using the crowd for testing. For example, at a crowdsourcing level, the government of India has already showcased recently how it could leverage the crowd. It invited the community to help design its symbol for the Indian currency—the Indian rupee—in 2010. The contest was won by an IIT Bombay postgraduate student, Udaya Kumar, showing the power of leveraging the crowd in various forms, in this case, crowd creation (Figure 9.1).

6. **Crowd testing will help students strengthen their resumes.** Crowd testing will become synonymous with self-initiated internships and projects, for students showcasing their proactiveness and additional skills, compared to others who do not take this route. This will help them strengthen their resumes, whether for future education or for employment opportunities.

Figure 9.1 Crowdsourcing competition organized by government of India.[50]

Business Trends

1. **Service level agreements (SLAs) at a soft level will be used.** It is very tricky to implement service level agreements in full rigor in crowdsourcing assignments because the crowd is engaged with you and your brand out of its own will and discretion. There is no formal binding for it to continue with you for a specific period of time. At the same time, organizations implementing crowdsourced testing will want to look for ways to introduce some discipline in the overall process to ensure they are able to get a regular flow of consistent input from the crowd. So, the service level agreements will have to be customized to be applied at a soft level, helping create the required level of discipline to differentiate the trusted crowd from the rest. These will largely be requirements around communication and response time, the level of detail in the reported bugs, the kind of bugs, etc.

2. **Internal buy-in for crowdsourced testing will go up.** As crowdsourced testing becomes more mature with increased use, process optimizations, and case studies to demonstrate value, successes, and learnings, there will be an increased internal buy-in for using this method more actively for software testing and quality assurance. The concerns and challenges that we discussed earlier on, including resistance from shareholders, will automatically give way to newer crowdsourced testing projects.

3. **Crowdsourced management teams, like vendor management teams, will be built.** As of today, most organizations, especially the larger ones that deal with external vendors, have vendor management teams to handle the management effort, including contracts, payments, invoices, etc. This is a formal discipline of its own. However, crowdsourced testing is not of a scale that necessitates a management team of its own from an administration standpoint. However, as the numbers here go up, this will in the future warrant a team of its own to handle crowd nondisclosure agreements (NDAs), possible crowd background checks, crowd tester payments, etc.

4. **Newer payment models will emerge.** As of today, the most popular payment model, if paid crowdsourced testing projects are undertaken, is pay per bug or pay per valid bug, so it becomes a straightforward value-based remuneration for the crowd tester. In some sense, this is a soft SLA in itself. However, as a trusted crowd team emerges where enough confidence is built in their work, although they are not closely monitored or co-located with the rest of the team, newer payment models around pay per hour or pay per fixed project may also emerge. This will make the payment processing relatively easier and will be able to attract more crowd testers; however, this cannot be done for everyone. This can only be done for the trusted crowd with whom the organization has adequately worked with in the past and there is some mutual agreement in place, although it may not be a written and signed document, unlike in regular employment opportunities.

5. **Crowdsourced testing will become a platform to find good full-time employees.** Like what we said earlier, that students will be able to strengthen their profiles with crowd testing assignments, crowdsourced testing will be a good platform for employers to find good full-time employees, making it a win-win for both the organization and the crowd tester. The crowd platform will become a live interview playing field for organizations to gauge their testers and see which ones are really good to offer jobs to. Companies such as Amazon and Google have already been doing this to some extent, and this will become even more popular and commonly used in the coming years.

6. **There will be a lot more legal scrutiny in place.** As more payment-based crowdsourced testing projects take shape, internal audits and legal scrutiny around them will be necessitated to ensure the right use of the organization's funds. As mentioned earlier, this will also become part of the crowdsourced administration management team working with the legal department to ensure the required compliances have been taken care of and the required financial checks and balances have been implemented, including handling international payments for crowd testers that are located in different geographies.

Technology Trends

One of the major reasons for crowdsourced testing's growth in recent years, compared to in, say, the late 1990s or early 2000s, is directly linked to technology advancements. Specific technology trends and advancements have made newer techniques such as crowdsourced testing more feasible in connecting with the crowd. In the absence of these advancements, the concept would have been more of a theory than a practical implementation or, at the most, a limited form of implementation in the shape of beta testing.

The major technology drivers that have tremendously helped crowdsourced testing grow include:

1. **Global Internet penetration:** This is one major driver for crowdsourced testing. While a large percentage of the global population still lacks Internet access, its proliferation in the last decade is mind-boggling. Despite this mind-boggling growth, the number still stands only at 34%, which leaves a huge potential of another 66% that the Internet reach can possibly expand into.[29] Product companies and service providers are exploring newer and more powerful ways to expand Internet speeds as well as reach. As of this writing, Google is exploring its balloon services, Project Loon, to allow for Internet access in the remotest areas of the world to help expand global Internet penetration.[30]

2. **Growth in mobile computing:** As of 2013, there were 6.8 billion mobile subscriptions globally.[31] Mobile computing is an interesting phenomenon. It has been a reason why more crowdsourced testing has been necessitated, as not all testing can be done in-house. At the same time, it is also the device that the crowd uses that has enabled a better connection network between the crowd seeker (organization) and the community. So, it has been a significant trigger in creating the demand as well as meeting the supply for crowdsourced testing

3. **Growth in social computing:** Similar to mobile computing, social computing is also yet another major trigger that has fueled both the demand and supply for crowdsourced testing. Applications going social need the community to test them

from a diverse background, creating the demand for crowd-sourced testing. At the same time, they, as well as the other product and service companies, are able to better reach the masses to let them know about themselves and invite them to test using social platforms, helping address the demand and bring in the supply of crowdsourced testers. For example, Facebook is a major platform that several organizations use to conduct polls, surveys, ask for crowd votes, etc. The linkage between Internet penetration, mobile usage, social computing, and the end community is so strong that this bond will only further enhance crowdsourced testing in the years to come.

4. **Growth in cloud computing:** This is another prime reason attributing to the growth of crowdsourced testing, and it will continue to prove a trend in the coming years. Due to the deeper penetration of cloud computing and the growth in sophisticated feature sets, organizations are able to better share their builds and products to reach the community at large and also mitigate concerns around security by using concepts such as virtual private cloud. This helps them not just reach the masses, but reach them in a more safe and secure manner, enhancing the community's and the organization's trust in the crowdsourced testing model.

End User Trends

1. **Crowdsourced testing will beef up end user confidence in the product and serve as a neutralizing agent in product quality.** As more crowdsourced testing is adopted by organizations and end users see the results of it through a product of better quality, their confidence in the product and resultant market acceptance will go up. This is a great facelift for product companies in helping expand their user base, along with an element of fear that if they do not do well, the crowd itself will spread the message, affecting not only their potential user base, but also the existing base. Thus, the crowd will serve as a neutralizing body of people to spread not just the good, but also the bad and the ugly, forcing organizations to increasingly

focus on quality. A crowd's test results that have been incorporated in the product will be an added certification to the end user base that someone from its own community (of end users) has represented them, tested the product, and provided the feedback. This will further enhance the product's acceptance in the marketplace.

2. **End users will become more vocal in sharing their feedback with the product organization.** As crowdsourced testing becomes more widely used, end users who are not necessarily part of the crowdsourced test team will all of a sudden become more vocal in sharing their feedback (both positive and areas where the product can improve), because they now have increased confidence that the organization really values community feedback. This is the ideal state for an organization to reach, where a group of end users, not tagging themselves as crowd testers, voluntarily share their feedback on the product. Such feedback coming in, which may traditionally be reviewed by a support group, can now include a crowdsourced test management team member too, to make the triage more effective, helping channel such feedback points into the crowdsourced testing feedback pipeline.

Crowdsourced testing definitely has a lot of interesting impending growth areas (aka trends), as we looked at from various viewpoints. That said, it is also important to reiterate that while this growth will be significant, it will not or cannot gobble the traditional software testing models, including the core internal team and any outsourced or a contracted team's testing efforts. As crowdsourced testing matures in the coming years, organizations will become more seasoned in leveraging it and customizing it to their needs and will be able to draw the right balance between all these various engagement models in releasing a product or exceptional quality to the end users. After all, crowdsourced testing is "by the people, for the people, and of the people," so the people element will continue to be held high in taking their input and giving back to them in the form of a better product with enhanced quality.

So, what next at this time? You may say, "I have now understood crowdsourced testing in all its glory, including its strengths and weaknesses, how to apply it in a live project, how to build a career in crowdsourced testing, and what the future looks like." Well, there is one more piece to this pie that we want to leave you with—a piece that may take shape in the coming years, which if it does, will be a great facelift to crowdsourced testing as a whole. This is the piece of building an ecosystem around crowdsourced testing, where we need to understand what is an ecosystem, why do we need it, and how it is relevant to crowdsourced testing. For more details on this, see Chapter 10, the concluding chapter of this book. This is a trend that will cut across all four areas we discussed above—market, business, technology, and end user—and tie them together. This will be that one trend that will altogether be able to take crowdsourced testing into a completely new level of acceptance and implementation; to read our take on how this trend will shape up, let's move on to the next chapter.

Did You Know?[D-8]

Gartner's prediction is that by 2017 over 50% of consumer goods producers will get 75% of innovation and R&D through crowdsourced solutions. While we looked at trends specific to crowdsourced testing over the next few years, do you know what the predictions for crowdsourcing are specific to 2014? Here's a bulleted list of those predictions:

- Managers will need crowdsourcing on resumes.
- Crowdsourcing will boost bottom lines.
- The crowdsourcing ecosystem will blossom (our take on this, specific to the testing discipline, is detailed in Chapter 10).
- The crowdsourcing industry will consolidate.
- Crowdsourcing will change real people's lives.

10

BUILDING AN ECOSYSTEM AROUND CROWDSOURCED TESTING

We have the crowd.
We are aware of crowdsourcing.
We are seeing an increase in crowd testing assignments.
But where is the ecosystem?

What is an ecosystem? Defined in layman terms, it is a complex and diverse set of interactions that happen between multiple entities, both living and nonliving, in an environment. Despite all the attention, research, and application that has gone into crowdsourcing in recent years, there are some compelling questions that we are faced with at the end of the day:

- How easy is it for someone new to apply crowdsourced testing to address his or her needs?
- How easy is it for anyone out there to find an assignment in crowdsourced testing?

Having read this book so far, you should now understand the various angles of crowdsourcing, including its practical application in a project. However, given the bright future this discipline holds, what we need to additionally look at is how we can build an ecosystem to tie together the various disparate crowdsourced testing solutions and resources as of today. We live in a time where technology has eased communication significantly and has brought the world together. As players in a crowdsourced testing space, wouldn't it be nice if we start thinking about how to build and contribute to an ecosystem on crowdsourced testing that would help everyone involved get better returns on their investment? We want to close this book

143

with this thought, that we can get everyone involved in not just using crowdsourced testing, but thinking about such an ecosystem, which will hopefully be a reality in a few years time. If you were to ask if such an ecosystem is completely lacking as of today, we would say no. There are portions of it out there in the market, but they are all so disparate, addressing the needs of just a few organizations, and not necessarily globally visible. We will take our own case here. In Chapter 5, we talked about a crowdsourced testing platform that we have built at QA InfoTech that helps us connect with the crowd as well as with our clients. This may be one small step toward building such a larger ecosystem. Before we go into the individual pieces in greater detail, let's understand what a crowdsourced testing ecosystem is and what questions it can help address.

A crowdsourced testing ecosystem will connect disparate solutions that exist today and in the future toward building an interactive, informed, and accessible set of resources toward the successful completion of crowdsourced testing assignments. This could include resources such as:

- Crowd testers
- Crowd seekers
- A platform (potentially open source) that the crowd and the crowd seekers leverage
- Best practices (aka a common knowledge repository on crowdsourced testing), including legal considerations and engagement models
- Crowdsourced testing tools, including strongly looking at the option of the crowd's BYOD (bring your own device)

You may ask: Why do we need an ecosystem? Is this how other concepts such as outsourcing grew? The fact is that the reach of crowdsourcing is much larger than the reach of any other testing concept. It is growing virally and has the power to connect to remote global corners. Also, the value of crowdsourced testing will grow only through such enhanced connections. Given these inherent characteristics of crowdsourced testing, the need for an ecosystem is much more here. Such an ecosystem will help this concept further mature into a valuable practice aiding software testing, as opposed to a limited application with pockets of success in the absence of such as ecosystem.

Let's now look at each of these components in greater detail to see why and how they will play an important part in the crowdsourced testing ecosystem.

Crowd Testers

These people are the heart line of crowdsourced testing. Crowdsourced testing has become so popular primarily because of the crowd and the valuable feedback it provides on the products under test. First, is crowd tester the right name to refer to such a person, because most often the individual is not a tester? He may be a tester, but more importantly, he is an actual or a potential user or domain expert of the product, which is why he is sought after by the crowd employers. However, since in some shape or form he is executing a testing activity, whether or not he is a professionally trained tester, we will call him a crowd tester. Crowd testers are rising in number by the day and are made up of people of varying skills and backgrounds. If we look at some of the core questions that crowd testers have, they are largely around:

1. How do I find who needs crowdsourced testing help?
2. How do I find the right crowd employer that aligns with my needs and goals—for example, my working hours, my areas of work interest, and my intent to do this assignment with a goal of winning a testing gig?
3. If this is not like formal employment, what kind of negotiation should I do with an organization before I start crowd testing?
4. Are there people similar to me in the market that I can connect and interact with?
5. Will I be given any resources to work with or should I be using my own devices?

Wouldn't having and being a part of an ecosystem be nice to take care of these questions and help you be involved with the crowdsourced testing community?

Crowd Seekers

Just as the crowd tester forms the heart line of crowdsourced testing, the crowd employer is also a critical piece of the pie. Without this group of people, even if we had a bunch of several interested crowd testers, nothing would be accomplished. We are seeing more and more employers understand the value of crowdsourced testing and beginning to use it, but this number is still constrained due to various reasons. A few of those compelling reasons are:

1. How do I find the right crowd for my needs?
2. More importantly, how do I find, build, and retain a trusted crowd that is not spying on my product but has the right intention to help improve my product quality? Are there any background checks that need to be done on crowd testers?
3. What kind of a platform exists or should I build to carry on crowdsourced testing that will integrate seamlessly with my internal development platform?
4. What kinds of access should I be giving my crowd testers to encourage transparency, yet having a hold on my privacy?

Yet again, wouldn't having and being a part of an ecosystem be nice to take care of these questions and help you be involved with the crowdsourced testing community?

The Platform

Software testing is a mature discipline in the software development world. It has the right platforms that organizations have been using—be they commercial, open source, or homegrown in nature. Software testing is an important component of the application life cycle management (ALM) suites, giving testers the right platform to understand product requirements, design tests, log execution results, and file defects, and to stay connected with the rest of the team, whether local or remote. Such a platform for crowdsourced testing is lacking as of today. You may ask, why not leverage the same platform as that of core software testing? It is not impossible; however, it cannot be leveraged as is, since the core platform has a lot of internal dependencies and secure information that cannot be shared with an external crowd. Taking cues from such existing platforms, a new platform for crowdsourced testing has to evolve. Ideally, this needs to be an open-source platform that will provide an opportunity for the crowd and crowd seekers to customize and improvise to align with their needs. This is a platform that will provide the crowd and crowd seekers access to the following:

1. A dashboard for crowd seekers to come post their crowd testing projects.
2. A provision for the crowd to register to specific projects.
3. A discussion room for the crowd seekers and crowd to communicate (especially when they are remote) to ensure there is alignment, especially in projects where you need a selected and trusted crowd to work with. This could be a group discussion room or a 1:1 discussion room, depending on the needs of the crowd testing assignment.
4. A platform that gives you specific input and requirements that will help you understand the product and testing requirements for the required levels, once you are within a specific project.
5. A defect management system, not as elaborate as in a core testing effort, but with the basic defect parameters (such as title, description, actual and expected results, steps to reproduce, and test configuration used). This is a system that the crowd seeker will use to triage and resolve defects and send them back to the crowd if it needs to regress them. If the crowd is not tasked with regression, this is a platform to at least keep it posted on the status of the defect, promoting overall transparency in the testing process.
6. A system that has hooks with the required communication systems, for example, Wiki and Skype, to talk to the crowd as needed over the course of the testing effort.
7. A dashboard to keep the crowd in a project informed on what areas to focus on, if any, how other crowd members are faring, what kind of defects are coming in, what effect these have on product quality, etc.
8. A dashboard to explain how an individual crowd tester has performed, what remuneration is due to him, if any, details around payment, etc.

We don't have such a universal platform as of today, but individual organizations are creating them to address their own needs. For example, in Chapter 5 we presented the crowdsourced testing platform we built at QA InfoTech to address our needs. Such a solution needs to scale to address the needs of the crowdsourced testing community at large, and preferably be open source to create a standardized executional workflow. Such a platform will alleviate a lot of the overhead for both the crowd seeker and the employer, making them focus on the core of this task, which is to get valuable product feedback from the crowd, rather than focusing on the operational logistics.

The thing to keep in mind is that the questions above can be solved in isolation. There are several for-profit organizations that have been carrying out crowdsourced testing for some years now, and there are valuable lessons we can learn from their experience. We must indeed commend them for having helped bootstrap crowdsourced testing, giving it the initial global attention it deserves. However, as newer players start getting into this mix, wouldn't it be nice to have an open-source kind of a community or a forum that houses this ecosystem, making crowdsourced testing a true "by the people, for the people, and of the people" relationship? That is the idea we are trying to inculcate in your mind at the end of this book, to see how each of us as good Samaritans of the crowdsourced testing community can help this practice mature and benefit everyone involved.

Common Knowledge Repository on Crowdsourced Testing

While there is some information available on the Internet on what crowdsourced testing is and how it works, it is not detailed enough to guide a team that is new to this practice. That was one of the main reasons we wanted to write this book, to share our experiences with you and give you go-to material on implementing a crowdsourced testing project end to end. While it is nice to retain the free-flow style of execution in crowdsourced testing because that unleashes the crowd's creativity at its best, it is important to understand how this whole model works. It is important to know what the model's strengths and limitations are, when to apply it, how and where to apply it, what legalities are involved in executing a crowd testing project, what are the various engagement models in which you can work with the crowd on, etc. Such a repository could also be a forum for the crowd to share its experiences, case studies, learnings, and ask questions, if any. This could be a database of its own, residing in the platform we talked about in the previous section.

Tools to Help with the Crowdsourced Testing Effort

We already talked about communication tools and how they could form part of the crowdsourced testing platform. Typically, you do not want to handhold the crowd with tools that you would provide your internal team—for example, tool to use up the device memory, tool to generate test credit cards, tools to generate test accounts, etc., because herein you want this test effort to be as realistic as possible to how the end user would be using your product after release. After all, most of these are real end users, so you want to allow them to use the product in all its true grandeur without any interruptions from the product team side. However, the crowd would benefit from some productivity tools, such as screen video capture tools, a tool that can quickly scan the device it is using to collect details you may need, etc. At QA InfoTech we are currently working on an automated lab on a cloud framework that will down the line help us add end user devices to our cloud pool to maximize device usage. Such solutions could also be built upon in the future in these crowdsourced testing assignments. For example, the crowd seeker needs an application tested from the Africa geography on an Android device. It has found a crowd tester in Africa, but that person does not have an Android device, whereas a crowd tester in India does. If he is able to connect his device to the cloud and allow the tester in Africa to use it, it solves everyone's needs, and the device owner may herein be given some rental remuneration.

All of the above are great things to have, to ease the overall crowdsourced test execution process. However, these are easier said than done. These are right now just at the envisioning stage and have several considerations around security, performance, connectivity, etc., to be addressed before they become a reality. However, how can we reach the treetop if we don't aim for the stars? That is the whole goal of this chapter, to think big to empower a bright future for crowdsourced testing and provide cues on what might provide the springboard for the crowdsourced testing community a few years from now.

Let us look at this pictorially to get a better understanding of what this ecosystem will look like (see Figure 10.1).

Once such an ecosystem is built, it will be a self-correcting system that does not need a lot of maintenance by a given individual

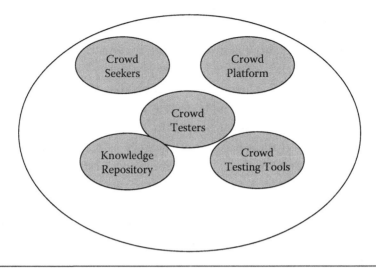

Figure 10.1   Envisioning an ecosystem for crowdsourced testing.

or a group. Everyone involved will take care of their interactions with the other entities in the group, stay updated as far as their profiles go, and help other entities stay updated (for example, make updates to the knowledge repository periodically), making it a true ecosystem and helping crowdsourced testing reach new heights in the years to come.

Who Is Responsible for Building This Ecosystem?

This is not an easy question to answer. There is no straightforward answer. There is no one single organization or individual who will be responsible for building the ecosystem. It needs to be a collective effort with the community coming together to promote this. What is heartening to see is that crowdsourcing and crowdsourced testing are becoming important topics of discussion in conferences in recent years. Specific conferences that solely focus on crowdsourcing are being arranged globally. Hopefully the initiative will be taken in such places to help this ecosystem see the light of the day. The goal to introduce this in the concluding chapter in this book is to introduce you to this idea and get you thinking on how you, as an enthusiastic participant of the crowdsourced testing community, can contribute to the shaping of this ecosystem.

What to Watch for as We Let the Ecosystem Develop

While we harp on the need for a crowdsourced testing ecosystem, there are cons of bringing in too much formality into this whole process. Crowdsourced testing gets most of its value and charm from the free-flow style of test execution and realistic end user experience that the users bring to the table. The ecosystem should only be an aid in bringing out the crowd's best by pointing it to the right resources, helping it with the needed tools, helping connect the crowd testers with crowd seekers, etc. It should at no point become mandating on how and what the crowd should do. If such a situation arises, the trust that all entities have in the ecosystem will fall apart, and the system itself will begin to disintegrate. To avoid such a scenario, we will need arbitrators or moderators to control how this ecosystem takes shape, helping drive back the value to the crowd testers and seekers. Again, all of these are still probably a few years out, but now is the time for us to start discussing such an ecosystem and explicitly using crowdsourced testing in possible ways to benefit the community at large. We truly hope this book has given you the required ammunition to dive into crowdsourced testing, whether you are a crowd seeker or a tester. We are very excited for what is in store for crowdsourced testing and are sure so are you. Let's be a change agent in helping crowdsourced testing mature and bloom into a practice that is here to stay for many more years to come.

Did You Know?[D-10]

We talked earlier about how an ecosystem around crowdsourcing will start taking shape in 2014. More specifically, in this chapter we talked about an ecosystem around crowdsourced testing. Speaking of the industry at large, there are isolated efforts that are under way to build such ecosystems at a crowdsourcing level. For example, did you know that KPMG has a crowdsourcing platform that it has built to work across domains and to provide its own consulting services on top of it? It is called Crowd Connection, and is said to be more powerful than standard market research methods that have been traditionally adopted. It will be exciting to see more such platforms evolve, not just commercially, but also the open-source way, and then integrate together into an ecosystem with the required tools, processes, and human element (i.e., the crowd users themselves).

References

1. http//www.slideshare.net/ConfCrowdsourcing2011/brazil-slides-july-2-2012.
2. http://thinkexist.com/quotation/before_the_beginning_of_great_brilliance-there/10821.html.
3. http://www.senatehouselibrary.ac.uk/2013/07/24/crowdsourcing-and-history-or-crowdsourcing-history/.
4. http://www.crowdsource.com/blog/2013/08/the-long-history-of-crowdsourcing-and-why-youre-just-now-hearing-about-it/.
5. http://www.alchemyofchange.net/crowd-wisdom-test/.
6. www.merriam-webster.com/dictionary/crowdsourcing.
7. http://crowdsourcing.typepad.com/cs/2006/06/crowdsourcing_a.html.
8. http://www.crowdsourcing-blog.org/wp-content/uploads/2012/02/Towards-an-integrated-crowdsourcing-definition-Estell%C3%A9s-Gonz%C3%A1lez.pdf.
9. http://en.wikipedia.org/wiki/Crowdsourcing.
10. References from the book *The Wisdom of Crowds*, by James Suroweicki.
11. http://www.chaordix.com/2009/08/eight-principles-to-successful-crowdsourcing/.
12. http://mashable.com/2012/04/05/jobs-act-signed/.
13. http://www.alumnifutures.com/2012/07/crowdsourced.html.
14. http://www.techwell.com/2013/11/how-bug-bounty-programs-deliver-savings-and-security.
15. http://arxiv.org/ftp/arxiv/papers/1203/1203.1468.pdf.
16. http://www.setheliot.com/blog/software-test-professionals-conference-2011/.
17. http://www.techwell.com/2013/11/there-recommended-duration-time-user-facing-test.

18. http://www.globaldialoguecenter.com/pdf/leadership-by-example/5-370-LEADERSHIP-BEST-PRACTICESfromParticipants.pdf.
19. https://wiki.yoctoproject.org/wiki/Bugzilla_Configuration_and_Bug_Tracking.
20. http://www.vincelombardi.com/quotes.html.
21. http://quarry.stanford.edu/webinars/101215apm.pdf.
22. http://www.pm4girls.elizabeth-harrin.com/2013/02/winning-stakeholder-support-when-time-and-energy-are-limited/.
23. http://www.goodreads.com/author/show/5741.Stacy_Schiff.
24. http://www.goodreads.com/work/quotes/12020129.
25. http://info.lionbridge.com/rs/lionbridge/images/Enterprise%20Crowdsourcing%20Webinar%20PDF.pdf.
26. http://www.ideaconnection.com/blog/2012/02/new-report-crowd-sourcing-enjoys-spectacular-growth-crowdsourcing-enjoys-spectacular-growth/#sthash.NkgaY8iS.VPPUZ0cn.dpbs.
27. http://techcrunch.com/2012/12/08/asias-secret-crowdsourcing-boom/.
28. http://www.prnewswire.com/news-releases/crowdfunding-market-grows-81-in-2012-crowdfunding-platforms-raise-27-billion-and-fund-more-than-one-million-campaigns-finds-research-firm-massolution-201911701.html.
29. http://www.internetworldstats.com/stats.htm.
30. http://www.google.com/loon/.
31. http://mobithinking.com/mobile-marketing-tools/latest-mobile-stats/a.
32. http://www.benjerry.org/activism/inside-the-pint/do-the-world-a-flavor/.
33. http://www.behance.net/gallery/Keep-It-Coolatta-2-Flavor-Boogaloo/11162789.
34. http://mashable.com/2009/09/08/vitamin-water-flavor-creator/.
35. http://www.simexchange.com/frontpage.php.
36. http://www.hobotraveler.com/jokes-sent-to-andy/coca-cola-salesman-in-saudi-arabia.php.
37. http://www.goodreads.com/quotes/384300-practice-doesn-t-make-perfect-practice-reduces-the-imperfection.
38. http://blog.programmableweb.com/2009/07/16/microsoft-shuts-down-its-popfly-mashup-tool/.
39. http://mvp.microsoft.com/en-us/default.aspx.
40. http://www.susannebarrett.com/p/my-essay-grading-service.html.
41. http://livemocha.com/pages/who-is-in-the-livemocha-community/.
42. http://www.designcontest.com/blog/why-crowdsourcing/.
43. Inputs from Ross Smith, Director of Test, Microsoft Corporation.
44. http://www.42projects.org/docs/The_Future_of_Work_is_Play.pdf.
45. http://softwaretestingfundamentals.com/software-testing-quotes/.
46. http://management.about.com/od/metrics/a/Measure2Manage.htm.
47. http://www.goodreads.com/quotes/115544-a-leader-is-a-dealer-in-hope.
48. http://www.goodreads.com/quotes/63089-the-world-is-full-of-willing-people-some-willing-to.

49. http://www.goodreads.com/quotes/21535-the-journey-of-a-thousand-miles-begins-with-a-single.
50. http://blog.designcrowd.co.in/article/177/how-india-crowdsourced-the-rupee—interview-with-udaya-kumar.
C-1. https://www.facebook.com/publications/514128035341603.

"Did You Know?" Section References

D-1. http://explore2win.blogspot.in/2012/10/what-is-crowdsourcing.html.
D-2. http://crowdsourcingweek.com/how-coca-cola-and-energizer-are-boosting-their-media-roi-through-crowdsourcing/.
D-3. http://www.playthework.com/search/label/Crowdsourcing.
D-4. http://econsultancy.com/blog/62504-eight-brands-that-crowd-sourced-marketing-and-product-ideas.
D-5. http://crowdsourcingweek.com/group-brainstorming-60-years-on/.
D-6. http://crowdsourcingweek.com/crowd-engagement-strategies/.
D-7. https://wiki.aalto.fi/pages/viewpage.action?pageId=75661920.
D-8. http://crowdsourcingweek.com/five-predictions-for-crowdsourcing-in-2014/.
D-9. http://www.innocentive.com/blog/2013/10/18/5-examples-of-companies-innovating-with-crowdsourcing/.
D-10. http://www.kpmg.com/uk/en/services/advisory/management-consulting/pages/crowd-connection.aspx.
D-11. http://news.cision.com/connect-communications—inc-/r/13-fun—-fascinating-facts-not-to-be-feared-on-crowdsourcing,c9246392.
D-12. http://yannigroth.com/2013/12/31/to-end-2013-some-stats-from-the-crowdsourcing-timeline/.

Quote Reference

Q-1. http://www.goodreads.com/quotes/56863-none-of-us-is-as-smart-as-all-of-us.

Index

A

Accessibility testing, 44
ALM suites. *See* Application life
cycle management suites
Amazon, use of crowdsourcing, 9
Antipiracy requirements, 101–102
Application life cycle management
suites, 146

B

Best practices, 64–75
communication, 73
content files, 67
empowerment, 72–73
feedback, 67–69
functionality of product, 65–66
internal team feedback, 66
manager, 72
motivational tasks, 74–75
motivator identification, 74
outsourced efforts, 67
stakeholder approval, 74
subject matter expertise, 69–70
team creation, 71–72

Beta testing projects, 124
Business trends, 137–138

C

Career, crowdsourced testing,
120–122
Case studies, defect management,
95–96
Challenges
crowdsourced testing, 55–62
defect management, 86–89
Citroen, 31
Closure, filing defects, 91–92
Cloud computing, 140
Cloud platform, 24
Common knowledge repository, 148
Communication, 73, 93, 107
Compatibility testing, 46
Confidence, end user, 140–141
Confidentiality, 101–102
Content files, 67
Continuity of efforts, 125
Core testing tasks, 53–55
Cost of quality, 119
Creation of crowd, 14–16

Crowd, traits of, 6–9
  attitude, testing, 7–8
  curiosity, 8
  end user mind-set, 6–7
  enhanced observational skill, 8
  inquisitive nature, 8
  questioning mind-set, 8–9
CrowdsourceTesting.com, 25
CrowdSourcing.org, 24–25
Curiosity, 8

D

Dailycrowdsource.com, 24
Dedication, 126
Defect management, 85–97
  case studies, 95–96
  challenges, 86–89
  communication, 93
  defect tracking, 94–95
  defined, 85–86
  filing defects, 88
    formal closure, 91–92
  following up, 94
  location, crowd testers, 90
  objectivity, 89
  overhead, defect management
    as, 89
  proactive decision-making, 87–88
  processes, 87, 93
  triage team, 91
Defining crowd, 2
Defining crowdsourcing, 9, 11
Delegation process, 25
Devices inventory, 123
Diverse platforms, 24
Diversity, 124
Domain specialties, 123
DuPont, use of crowdsourcing, 9

E

Employment opportunities, 135
Empowerment, 72–73

End user representation, 26
End user trends, 140–142
End users, 100
Engagement models, 82–84
  payment, 83–84
Enhanced observational skill, 8
Environment-specific
  complexity, 52
Examples, crowdsourced testing,
  27–28
Exchange markets, 19
Expedia, 31–32
External crowd usability testing, 54
  backgrounds, 54
  cost, 54
  feedback, 54
  focus, 54
  interaction, 54
  number of participants, 54
  pros/cons, 54
  spammers, 54
  speed, 54
  vs. in-house, 54
External entities, 100–101
  community at large, 100
  end users, 100
  government, 100
  shareholders, 100
  social groups, 100
  suppliers, 100

F

Feedback, 54, 67–69, 141
Filing defects, 88
  formal closure, 91–92
Focus, 54
Follow-up, 94
Formal closure, filing defects,
  91–92
Formal *vs.* crowdsourced testing
  career, 121
Full-time employment, 138

Functional testing, 42–43
Functionality of product, 65–66
Funding, crowd, 20–21
Future developments, 131–142
  business trends, 137–138
  end user trends, 140–142
  market trends, 135–136
  technology trends, 139–140
Future work skills, 80–81

G

Global access, 133
Global Internet penetration, 139
Globalization testing, 45–46
Government, 100
Governmental interest, 136

H

History of crowdsourcing, 2–4
  software product development, 4
Hope, communication of, 81–82
Howe, Jeff, 11

I

Identification of stakeholder,
  104–105
Implementation, testing, 63–84
In-house *vs.* external crowd
  testing, 54
Independence in work, 121
Industry news, 126
Inquisitive nature, 8
Intellectual property, 52, 101–102
Internal buy-in, 137
Internal team feedback, 66
Internet penetration, 139

K

Knowledge repository, 148

L

Language skills, 123
Language usage, 81
Legal examination, 138
Leveraging crowdsourced testing, 42
  accessibility testing, 44
  compatibility testing, 46
  functional testing, 42–43
  globalization testing, 45–46
  performance testing, 44–45
  security testing, 45
  usability testing, 43–44
  user interface testing, 43
Levi's, 31
Limitations, crowdsourced test
  effort, 55–62
Location of crowd testers, 90

M

Management overhead, 101
Management team, 137
Managers, 72
Market trends, 135–136
Mind-set of end user, 6–7
Mobile computing, 139
Motivation, 102, 124–125
Motivational tasks, 74–75
Motivator identification, 74
Myths, 119–120

N

NDA. *See* Nondisclosure agreement
Netflix, use of crowdsourcing, 9
News, industry, 126
Nissan, 31
Nondisclosure agreement, 13
Nonprofit organizations, 100

O

Objectivity, 89
Observational skill, 8

Outsourced efforts, 67
Outsourcing, crowdsourcing,
    distinguished, 21–23
Overhead, 101
    defect management as, 89

P

Payment, 83–84
    models for, 138
Performance testing, 44–45
Platform, 11, 146–148
Popularity of crowdsourcing, 29–30
Preparation, crowdsourced testing,
    122–129
Privacy, 101–102
Proactive decision-making, 87–88

Q

Qualifications, crowdsourced tester,
    120–122
Quality control, 33–38, 49–62,
    102–103
    core testing tasks, 53–55
    environment-specific
        complexity, 52
    intellectual property, 52
    turnaround, 52–53

R

Registration, 122–123
Repository, common knowledge, 148
Representation of end user, 26
Resume building, 136
Rosenblatt, Gideon, 4

S

Security testing, 45
Service level agreements, 137
Shareholders, 100

Sizing industry, 131–133
SLAs. *See* Service level agreements
SME. *See* Subject matter expertise
Social computing, 139–140
Social groups, 100
Software product development, 4
Software testing, 33–47
    quality issues, 33–38
Spammers, 54
Special interest groups, 135–136
Sponsors' support, 104–108
Stakeholder approval, 74
Stakeholder identification, 104–105
Subject matter expertise, 25–26,
    69–70
Suppliers, 100
Support, 103–108

T

Team, 99–109
    antipiracy requirements, 101–102
    communication, 107
    confidentiality, 101–102
    creation of, 71–72
    external entities, 100–101
        community at large, 100
        end users, 100
        government, 100
        shareholders, 100
        social groups, 100
        suppliers, 100
    intellectual property, 101–102
    internal entities, 100
    management overhead, 101
    motivation, 102
    privacy, 101–102
    quality, 102–103
    sponsors' support, 104–108
    stakeholder identification, 104–105
    strategy, 105–106
    support, 103–104
    triage, 91

value from crowd, 101
vendor management, 137
Technology trends, 139–140
Testing effort, 23–26
Testing know-how, 25
Tools, crowdsourced testing, 149–150
Tracking defects, 94–95
Traits of crowd, 6–9
 attitude, testing, 7–8
 curiosity, 8
 enhanced observational skill, 8
 inquisitive nature, 8
 end user mind-set, 6–7
 questioning mind-set, 8–9
Transparency in work, 121
Triage expectations, 93
Triage team, 91
Trust, 135
Turnaround, 52–53

U

UI testing. *See* User interface testing
Usability testing, 43–44
User interface testing, 43

V

Value from crowd, 101
Varied forms, crowdsourcing, 12
Vendor management team, 137
Voting, 16–17

W

Wikipedia, use of crowdsourcing, 9
Wisdom of crowd, 18
The Wisdom of Crowds, 4
Work skills, 80

Y

Your Bank—Your Design Project, 31

Z

Zhubajie, 133